THE DIAMOND SUTRA &
THE SUTRA OF HUI NENG

The Diamond Sutra

and

The Sutra of Hui Neng

Translated by
A.F. Price and Wong Mou-Lam

With Forewords by
W.Y. EVANS-WENTZ, JOE MILLER
and CHRISTMAS HUMPHREYS

THE CLEAR LIGHT SERIES

SHAMBHALA   BOULDER

1969

Shambhala Publications, Inc.
1123 Spruce Street
Boulder, Colorado 80302

ISBN 0-87773-005-9

Published by arrangement with the
Buddhist Society, London

Distributed in the United States by *Random House, Inc.*
and in Canada by *Random House of Canada Ltd.*

Printed in the United States of America

FRONT COVER: *The Sixth Patriarch Cutting Bamboo*
by Liang K'ai

While he was still a layman, Hui-Neng, the Sixth Patri-arch of Zen, would go into the hills and cut firewood, which he brought on his back to sell in the town. One day, he had stopped to rest when he heard a monk re-citing the *Diamond Sutra* before a layman's home, and determined on the spot that he would take holy vows himself.

BACK COVER: *The Sixth Patriarch's Verse* by Torei

Hui-Neng, upon first entering a monastary, spent his days in the refectory treading away at the mill used for hulling rice. It was while he was doing so that he a-chieved enlightenment and wrote his famous verse. (See page 18 of *The Sutra of Hui-Neng.*)

This book is published in the *Clear Light Series* dedicated to W.Y. Evans-Wentz. The series is under the joint editorship of Samuel Bercholz & Michael Fagan.

Book One

The Diamond Sutra

CONTENTS

4

PREFACE

The Origin of the Text

The original of the Jewel of Transcendental Wisdom is a Sanskrit text called the *Vajrachchedikaprajñāpāramitā Sutra*. The *Vajrachchedika* (Diamond Cutter) is a small book belonging to the *Maha-Prajñāpāramitā* (Perfection of Transcendental Wisdom). It may be called a classic, a scripture, or a discourse, as all these three terms are comprehended in the Sanskrit word *Sutra*, which is the appellation given to the Sacred Books of the Buddhist Canon.

The Perfection of Transcendental Wisdom is one of many books in the great Canon of Mahayana (or Northern) Buddhism, and it is by far the largest, running into a great number of volumes. Many of the books of which this is made up are written in the form of dialogues between the Buddha and one or other of His chief disciples ; but in point of fact these dialogues are not likely to be records of actual discourses. The Buddha left no written testament, and though records were made from memory by His followers some years after His passing, many parts of the Northern Canon are of much later date. It is generally considered by the faithful that these later works enshrine the deep teachings of their Lord, and that these teachings were passed down orally from generation to generation amongst those elect who proved the truths for themselves by practice. Precisely why, and when, and by whom, this oral transmission came to be set down in symbols cannot be stated with certainty ; but research may provide these data at any moment.

The writings here concerned are generally considered to be the work of the profound and saintly thirteenth patriarch, Nagarjuna, who lived in the second century of the Christian era ; but it would seem wiser to take the view that there was a succession of authors and compilers extending over a period of several hundred years from the first century B.C.E. and that the Diamond Cutter was written in the fourth century C.E.

Although it forms so small a part of the Great Scriptures on the Perfection of Transcendental Wisdom, its importance lies in its being an epitome of the whole. It is therefore extremely profound and extremely subtle.

Chinese Versions

The Diamond Cutter was first translated into Chinese by Kumarajiva about 400 C.E., and he called it simply "The Diamond Sutra." It is recorded that Kumarajiva was a native of Kucha, an ancient state in Eastern Turkestan. When he was in his middle-age he travelled to Ch'ang-an and there engaged upon translation work which reached monumental proportions. His rendering of the Diamond Cutter is an exquisite classic which has taken popular precedence in China over subsequent translations made by Bodhiruchi, Paramartha, Hsuan-tsang, I-tsing and Dharmagupta.

One of the greatest difficulties with which Kumarajiva had to contend was the Sanskrit Buddhist idioms, the meanings of which could not be spontaneously evoked in the Chinese mind by the use of the characters of their language. For the most part these were dealt with by phonetical transliterations of the approximate Sanskrit sounds. For example, Prajnaparamita, which we have called "Perfection of Transcendental Wisdom," was set down as "*Pahn zhor por lore mee.*" It will be imagined that the liberal peppering of a classic with such sets of characters, which make no sense in themselves, added obscurity to the other difficulties of understanding it. As a result, highly-educated Chinese cannot comprehend these works without special study, and the diffusion of the Buddhist treasury was accordingly inhibited. Upon seeing the beneficent effect which Buddhism has had upon Chinese thought and culture, one is tempted to wonder how much greater good it might have done had it been possible to remove this stumbling-block.

English Versions

There are four comparatively well-known English translations. (1) Professor Max Muller's, a rather literal translation from the Sanskrit, included in *The Sacred Books of the East ;* (2) Dr. Samuel Beal's, published in the *Journal of the Royal Asiatic Society ;* (3) Mr. William Gemmell's, an interpretive translation unfortunately now out of print ; (4) Dr. D. T. Suzuki's, an incomplete translation of literal character, included in a Japanese publication unobtainable for the time being. All except Professor Max Muller's were made from Kumarajiva's text.

The Present Version

It is to make the work once more accessible to the general reader in a handy form that the present translation has been undertaken. A number of Commentary Notes have been added, but except where these endeavour to be technically informative they are intended to be suggestive rather than explanatory. They will have served their purpose if they show that the scripture is neither too abstruse to repay close study, nor too superficial to be worthy of it ; though both these opinions have been expressed concerning it.

In translating, the aim has been faithfulness to the spirit of the text by avoiding literal and interpretive extremes ; and an attempt has been made to demonstrate the universality of the Discourse by finding English equivalents for the Sanskrit terms. It is felt that too often in the past, translations of great scriptures have been confined to this school or that because of their technical terminology. Justification is therefore pleaded in the face of inadequacy, and the reader who is accustomed to using the original idioms in his thoughts will find these provided in the notes.

It gives me great pleasure to record my gratitude to the many friends who have rendered invaluable help. Among these I wish to mention Dr. W. Y. Evans-Wentz, Mr. John Blofeld, Dr. Edward Conze, Miss Clare Cameron, Mr. Christmas Humphreys, and Mr. L. F. Menzies Jones.

An Approach to the Diamond Sutra.

The reader who has heard the fame of this Buddhist scripture and quickly reads in the hope of finding arcane knowledge, is likely to be disappointed. We can say certainly that it was not the intention of the author to provide intellectual data. However, those who have many times carefully read and thoroughly meditated upon the sections in their proper order have found that the mind is re-oriented in a striking way. In the light of this re-orientation the problems of life assume different proportions, and a new and clearer perspective gradually takes the place of the old.

We have described the work as extremely profound and subtle. These qualities do not make for easy study, and after first reading, the newcomer may feel despondent about seeing more than a glimmer of light as to the meaning. But it should be realised that this ancient book does not belong to the class of flowing literature to which we are accustomed, conveying ideas as quickly as we can read. It can be read in an hour, but the thoughts which underlie its words are the outcome of centuries of genius.

Lao Tzu, Venerable Sage of China, said: "The journey of a thousand miles starts from beneath one's feet." Encouragement indeed! If we gain just a little insight we shall have found the beginning of a sure way. If we tread this way patiently and steadily it will lead us to the Place of Jewels.

A. F. PRICE.

Elmsett, Suffolk,
    1947

Bibliography

For The Diamond Cutter Sutra see :
    The Sacred Books of the East. Vol. 49. Edited by Max Muller. Clarendon Press.
    Journal of Royal Asiatic Society, 1864.
    The Diamond Sutra. By W. Gemmel. Kegan Paul Trench Trubner & Co., Ltd., O.P.
    A Manual of Zen Buddhism. By D. T. Suzuki. Eastern Buddhist Society Kyoto, 1935.
For an account of the Chinese Translators see :
    In the Footsteps of Buddha. By Rene Grousset. Routledge.

FOREWORD

———

ADDED ILLUMINATION FROM THE EAST

———

By Dr. W. Y. Evans-Wentz

"It is great joy to realize that the Path to Freedom which all the Buddhas have trodden is ever-existent, ever unchanged, and ever open to those who are prepared to enter upon it."—*Precepts of the Gurus*.

I: *The Rendering, the History, and the Significance of the Text.*

In presenting to the West this rendering of *The Jewel of Transcendental Wisdom*, Mr. Price reveals himself to be one of that noble band of translators and transmitters who in our time have added fresh effulgence to the Light born of the East.

From India, the Guru of the World, and the land wherein they first took written form, in Sanskrit, the *Prajñā-Pāramitā* Scriptures were carried into China, and from the Chinese version of one of their various epitomes issues this English version here before us, which is characterized by praiseworthy simplicity of phraseology and diction, clarity of exposition, and unusually valuable notes that serve as a quite necessary commentary.

In my own presentation of a still more epitomized version of *The Transcendental Wisdom*, contained in Book VII of *Tibetan Yoga and Secret Doctrines*, I have set forth a brief account of the history and esotericism of the *Prajñā-Pāramitā* Scriptures, which form a part of the third division of the Tibetan canon of Northern Buddhism, corresponding to the *Abhidhamma* of the Pali canon of Southern Buddhism. In the Tibetan block-print editions, the *Prajñā-Pāramitā* Scriptures ordinarily comprise twenty-one books, contained in one-hundred volumes of approximately one-thousand pages each. Of these voluminous texts there are numerous epitomes in various oriental languages, ranging from the original Sanskrit to Mongolian and Japanese. For Northern, or Mahāyānist, Buddhists, the *Prajñā-Pāramitā* Scriptures are the most precious and sacred of their canonical writings. Nāgārjuna, the thirteenth of the Buddhist Patriarchs, who flourished during the first half of the second century A.D., is credited with having been the first teacher publicly to teach the supreme doctrine of the Voidness as therein set forth. According to Nāgārjuna, the Dynasty of Buddhas, of whom the Buddha Shākya Muni is the representative in this epoch, first enunciated the doctrine of the Voidness, apparently in a purely esoteric manner, to highly advanced disciples. As our own text states, in Section XV, "The Tathāgata has declared this teaching for the benefit of initiates of the Great Way ; he has declared it for the benefit of initiates of the Supreme Way."

II : The Transcendence of the Doctrine of the Voidness.

Although the doctrine is now accessible to all pilgrims on the quest for truth, nevertheless, for many of them, as for the unenlightened multitude, it remains, in essence, esoteric. Until the Occident outgrows its adolescent assumption of intellectual and spiritual superiority over the Wise Men of the East, it will fail to understand, much less to profit by, the doctrine of the Voidness. Wherever progress is measured in terms of technology and not in terms of Right Understanding, the perfecting of the machine rather than of man will be the guiding ideal.

All supreme teachings, like these herein set forth, are for the purpose of emancipating man from worldly and conditioned existence; and, once man is thus emancipated, no need will he have for technological perfection. When the butterfly has escaped from the chrysalis state, has cast aside the cocoon prison house, its former state, when it was an earth-bound crawling caterpillar, has become obsolete. The world, however perfected it may become by means of utilitarian science, however utopian it may be made by human effort, can never be more, at best, than a state of chrysalism, preparatory to the incomparably greater state of *Nirvāna*.

Like the fabled frog who imagined the water in his well to be unsurpassed in depth and vastness and knew not of the deep, vast ocean, world-fettered men comprehend only the Small and know nought of the Great; they fail to comprehend the far-reaching significance of St. Paul's pronouncement: "The things that are seen are temporal; the things that are unseen are eternal."

III : *The Yoga of the Doctrine.*

The reading of no part of the *Prajñā-Pāramitā* Scriptures, whether in epitomized form, such as that before us, or in the full twenty-one volume form, can be profitably undertaken without profound seriousness. If these Scriptures be, as they purport to be, nothing less than a guide to the Other Shore, to transcendence

over all conditionedness, to a state of which no pre-
dication comprehensible to man immersed in the human
state is possible, it must follow that they cannot be
fruitfully studied by purely intellectual means. The
translator, too, has given necessary admonition of this.
The student should approach the doctrine of the Voidness
with a mind freed from all previously acquired intellect-
ualisms, particularly if these be occidentally shaped.
When the intent of the guidance set forth in our text
has been, to some degree, understood, it should be self-
evident that only by application of the deepest meditation
can the disciple hope to advance on the path leading to
super-human wisdom.

The yogic method of understanding these transcendent
teachings is itself transcendent ; as the text states, in
Section XIV, "The mind should be kept independent
of any thoughts which arise within it," or "If the mind
[when practising this yoga] depends upon anything,
it has no sure haven." All those who seek the consummation of Incomparable Enlightenment, as explained
in Sections II and III, even "Bodhisattva-Heroes, should
discipline their thoughts." Also, "no Bodhisattva who
is a real Bodhisattva cherishes the idea of an ego-entity,
a personality, a being, or a separated individuality."
As explained further, in Section XVII, "If a Bodhisattva
cherishes the idea of an ego-entity, a personality, a being,
or a separated individuality, he is, consequently, not a
Bodhisattva." Accordingly, as stated in Section XV,
"those who find consolation is limited doctrines involving the conception of an ego-entity, a personality, a
being, or a separated individuality, are unable to accept,
receive, study, recite, and openly explain this
Discourse."

14

In this insistence, repeated throughout the text, upon the doctrine of non-ego, of non-soul, the *Sutra* is unquestionably in full accord with the fundamental teaching of the Buddha, and is, thus, strictly Buddhistic, despite whatever may be argued against it otherwise by Buddhists of the Theravādin, or Southern, School.

In the practice of this yoga, there must be, as the text makes clear, detachment from the results of action, which is, equally, the teaching of the Indian *Bhagavad Gitā*. In Section IV, the practitioner is warned against even charitable acts performed with a view to attaining spiritual benefit: "In the practice of charity a Bodhisattva should be detached." There must be no dependence upon any formulated teaching, or doctrine, or enunication of truth ; for truth, being uncontainable and inexpressible "neither *is* nor is it *not*," as set forth in Section VII; "and this unformulated Principle is the foundation of the different systems of all the sages."

Salvation is not, contrary to what the multitude are taught to believe, purchasable by good works. It is not the giving away in charity of worldly treasures, however inconceivably great, that matters, but the practising and dissemination of the *Buddha Dharma*.

Throughout the *Sutra* runs the Buddha's denial of the reality of all predicable things, as of ego, or soul, of all appearances, likewise of merit, even of Liberation and Non-Liberation. As the Tibetan Gurus continue to teach their disciples, in the analysis of the fully enlightened mind no differentiation whatsoever is possible between *Nirvāna*, the Unborn, the Primordially Undifferentiated, the All-At-One-Ment, and the *Samsāra*, the Born, the Created, the Shaped, the Differentiated Cosmos. "The Perfection of Transcendental Wisdom"

15

itself is no more than a human concept; and, like the human mind that conceived it, is, therefore, "not really such." The Buddha Himself, as Subhuti perceives, "has nothing to teach." Although by means of Right Understanding, born of Right Meditation, man may conceive the idea of Fundamental Reality, it is, ultimately, for the Enlightened One, no more than a mental concept, is "merely a name." So, too, is Bodhisattvaship.

Nirvāna and the *Samsāra* are, for the mind of men, merely the ultimate pair of opposites; and, like all lesser pairs of opposites, of which are ego and non-ego, they are unreal. Only in the transcendent state, beyond the domain of opposites, is Truth realizable.

But "Truth is undeclarable"; and "an enunciation of Truth is just the name given to it," by unenlightened man, as taught in Section XXI. Goodness, likewise, "is merely a name," and like all else that the human mind conceives. "There is," as stated in Section IX, "no passing away nor coming into existence." Nothing is really acquired by attaining Enlightenment; the yogin merely transcends man's Realm of Ignorance wherein selfhood illusorily seems real. There actually are no beings to liberate, for there are, in fact, no beings; hence, the thought of liberating beings that are non-existent is purely illusory. The attaining of Buddhahood is not the attaining of anything; it is no more than the realization of something eternally and indestructibly potential in every living creature. Thus, there is no fundamental difference between one who is and one who is not a Buddha; a Buddha knows, and the non-Buddha does not know, that he is a Buddha. In the Full Awakening from the Dream of Existence, upon the attaining of Buddhahood, nothing is either lost or gained; there is only the realization of What has ever been beyond the grasp of mortal mind.

Thus is set forth suggestively, as far as the speech of world-fettered man can set it forth, the Doctrine of the Voidness, known in Sanskrit as *Shunyatā*.

In mentally descending from this supernal thought-realm of the Sages of the *Mahāyāna*, the Great Path, one returns to the human realm of illusion, in which the myriads of unemancipated men are born, wherein they struggle in the sorrows of an animal existence, and whence they depart at the dissolution of their physical bodies. Fettered to appearances, believing that what the senses perceive is alone real, the vast majority of mankind expend incarnation after incarnation in glamour-ous attachment to the world. Perhaps never before, since Earth became a man-bearing planet, has so much attention been given to the study of natural, or illusory, laws, to the application of physical science to purely worldly and transitory ends. Men forget that the chief purpose of being incarnate is not to exploit and conquer external nature, but to conquer the self, to evolve beyond the commonly-held concept of an in-dividualized personality, to transcend appearances, to realize the untenability and delusiveness of the doctrine of ego, or soul.

The quest for reality is unceasing so long as man is man. It is not by being led, as are the multitude, from sensation to sensation, and by wandering through innumerable incarnations with no consciousness of right direction, that Transcendental Wisdom is to be attained; or that the Supreme Goal, All-Understanding, the Final At-One-Ment, the ripened fruit of Yoga, is realiz-able. The Kingly, or Royal, Science is to be won only by entering into the Inner Sanctuary of the Body Temple.

IV. : The Winning of Merit and the Oriental Praise of Doctrines.

The criticism that our text over-stresses how merit may be won by following the *Prajñā-Pāramitā* teachings, appears to be based upon an incomplete understanding of the spiritual purport underlying the *Sutra* when evaluated as a whole ; the translator has suggested this to me, and rightly, I think. The merit to be won is not to be taken as being like a reward given by one person to another or by a god to a devotee, but rather as a virtue, already innate, developed, and made active, as the direct result of endeavour rightly applied, and by means of which karma inimical to progression on the path may be neutralized. Unless psychically beneficial results be attainable by practical application of these transcendent teachings, it is quite unlikely that the teachings would have survived in their completeness, as a highly-developed system of yoga, and be, as they are, widely practised until today, eighteen centuries after their compilation.

It is typically oriental to bestow what to the occidental seems to be extravagent praise on a highly-venerated book or even to exhibit proselytizing zeal on behalf of a doctrine. If, as a result of generations of testing by practice, a doctrine is found to be efficacious, a teacher is justified in extolling it in the same manner that a medical practitioner may extol a really excellent method of curing a disease. The Buddha, like the Christ, is often referred to as the Great Physician ; and He, too, spent a long lifetime extolling His remedy

18

for Ignorance, the *Dharma*. Similarly, and by way of illustration, and also, to serve as commentary here, may very rightly be applied to the *Prajñā-Pāramitā* Scriptures the praise given to the sacred *Biography* of Milarepa, Tibet's illustrious saint and pre-eminent yogin, whom his followers, of the Kargyütpa School, consider to be a second Buddha :—

"Through one's study and practice of this *Biography*, the Dynasty of Gurus will be fully satisfied ;
May it thus be a feast of delight to them who uphold the glory of the Dynasty of Gurus by living according to their commandments.

"In virtue of the Grace of this *Biography*, every sentient creature shall find relief from sorrow ;
May it thus be a feast of delight to all sentient creatures of the Three Planes [of the Universe]" (*)

In like manner, the Great Gurus of Tibet praise, as they should, the Buddha's *Dharma*, or Doctrine, of which the *Prajñā-Pāramitā* Scriptures represent a very important part :—

"The fact that there have arisen in the world those who have entered the Stream, those who will return to birth but once more, those who have passed beyond the need of further birth, and *Arhants*, and Self-Enlightened Buddhas and Omniscient Buddhas, showeth the virtue of the Holy *Dharma*." (†)

V : Human Birth and Its Mighty Opportunity.

As many of the sacred books of the East emphasize, for sentient beings a human birth is difficult to win ; as the Tibetan Teachers declare, "None but the foolish fritter away the mighty opportunity offered by having attained human birth." And, by such guidance as the *Prajñā-Pāramitā* teachings offer, this mighty opportunity is here made available to the disciple ; and the disciple alone must make the choice, whether to be, as are the multitude, enslaved to the world, or to be set free to begin the Higher Evolution.   In the words of the Sages,

"The greatest fault to be avoided is Ignorance.
To overcome the enemy Ignorance, one requireth Wisdom.
The best method of acquiring Wisdom is unfaltering endeavour
 [in yogically directed meditation]."   (‡)

Herein, then, have I been privileged to suggest, to all to whom this precious *Jewel of Transcendental Wisdom* may come, the need of putting its teachings to the test of practice, and, as they do so, to treasure continually whilst incarnate here on Earth the admonition of the Sages :—

"Time is fleeting, learning is vast ; no one knoweth the duration
 of one's life :
Therefore use the swan's art of extracting milk from water,
And devote thyself to the Most Precious Path."   (¶)

(*) Cf.   W. Y. Evans-Wentz, *Tibet's Great Yogi Milarepa* (Oxford University Press, 1928) page 302.
(†) Cf.   W. Y. Evans-Wentz, *Tibetan Yoga and Secret Doctrines* (Oxford University Press, 1935), page 94.
(‡) Cf.   W. Y. Evans-Wentz, *Tibetan Yoga and Secret Doctrines,* page 65.
(¶) *Ibid,* page 62.

"*Come Blessed One we pray Thee, roll the wheel of the dew-sweet Law—which is excellent in the beginning, excellent in the middle, and excellent in the end!*"

THE DIAMOND SUTRA

Section I. The Convocation of the Assembly

Thus have I heard. Upon a time Buddha
sojourned in Anathapindika's Park by Shravasti
with a great company of bhikshus, even twelve
hundred and fifty.

One day, at the time for breaking fast, the World-
honoured enrobed, and carrying His bowl made His
way into the great city of Shravasti to beg for His
food.   In the midst of the city He begged from door
to door according to rule.   This done, He returned
to His retreat and took His meal.   When He had
finished He put away His robe and begging bowl,
washed His feet, arranged His seat, and sat down.

Notes

Shravasti, "City of Wonders," was in Northern India near the
Nepalese border.   Today it is the village of Sahet-mahet, on the
banks of the R. Rapti.

A Bhikshu is a religious mendicant or friar of the Order founded
by Gautama, the Buddha.

Bibliography

For an account of Anathapindika's Park, called the Jeta Grove,
and how it came to be given to the Order, see : *Some Sayings of
the Buddha*. By F. L. Woodward. (Oxford Press.) P. 141
onwards.

Section II.   Subhuti Makes a Request

Now in the midst of the assembly was the Venerable Subhuti.   Forthwith he arose, uncovered his right shoulder, knelt upon his right knee, and, respectfully raising his hands with palms joined, addressed Buddha thus : World-honoured One, it is most precious how mindful the Tathagata is of all the Bodhisattvas, protecting and instructing them so well !   World-honoured One, if good men and good women seek the Consummation of Incomparable Enlightenment, by what criteria should they abide and how should they control their thoughts ?

Buddha said : Very good, Subhuti ! Just as you say, the Tathagatha is ever-mindful of all the Bodhisattvas, protecting and instructing them well. Now listen and take my words to heart : I will declare to you by what criteria good men and good women seeking the Consummation of Incomparable Enlightenment should abide, and how they should control their thoughts.

Said Subhuti : Pray, do, World-honoured One. With joyful anticipation we long to hear.

Notes

"Tathagata" is a title of the Buddha.   The Discourse itself later unfolds its meaning herein.

A Bodhisattva is an advancing devotee of Enlightenment. A vast and complex doctrine surrounds this difficult Sanskrit

Buddhist term. It is most commonly considered to be derived from *Bodhi*—Enlightenment, and *Sattva*—a being; but we prefer the view that *Sattva* is related to *sakta* or *satvan*, implying a spiritual hero.

Consummation of Incomparable Enlightenment = *Anuttara Samyak Sambodhi.*

Very good = *Sadhu.*

Bibliography

For an exhaustive essay on the Bodhisattva see : *The Bodhisattva Doctrine in Buddhist Sanskrit Literature.* By Har Dayal. (Kegan Paul.)

Section III.   The Real Teaching of the Great Way

Buddha said : Subhuti, all the Bodhisattva-Heroes should discipline their thoughts as follows : All living creatures of whatever class, born from eggs, from wombs, from moisture, or by transformation, whether with form or without form, whether in a state of thinking or exempt from thought-necessity, or wholly beyond all thought realms—all these are caused by Me to attain Unbounded Liberation Nirvana. Yet when vast, uncountable, immeasurable numbers of beings have thus been liberated, verily no being has been liberated. Why is this, Subhuti ? It is because no Bodhisattva who is a real Bodhisattva cherishes the idea of an ego-entity, a personality, a being, or a separated individuality.

Notes

Everyday thinking-processes belong to the state of limited and purblind self-consciousness. To detach the mind from self and unite it with Essence of Mind is the object of sound Yoga (Union). Patanjali defines Yoga as "Suppression of the transformations of the thinking principle."

The title *Buddha* means "Enlightened One" ; liberation is reached through Enlightenment. Liberation is not *of* a being, but *from* a being.

"Born from Moisture" is generally considered as referring to the lowest forms of animal life ; but it can be considered as symbolical. Water often has the mystical significance of Life at a higher level than the mundane world.

"Born by transformation" refers to heavenly birth ; Aupapadaka.

Creatures : (1) With form ; (2) without form ; (3) supravading thought necessity ; and (4) wholly beyond all thought realms, may be considered as applying respectively to the Six Kingdoms of the Wheel of Life and Death—viz., Gods, Titans, Men, Brutes, Elementals and Sufferers and Demons in Hell ; (2) the Arupa (Formless) States ; (3) Avriha, the thirteenth Brahmaloka ; and (4) Naivasamjna-anasamjnayatana.

The Great Way = Mahayana.
Bodhisattva-Heroes = B./Mahasattvas.
Unbounded Liberation Nirvana = Anupadhishesa.

Bibliography

A Manual of Buddhist Philosophy. W. Mcgovern (Kegan Paul).

The Yoga Sutras of Patanjali. Edited by Dvivedi. (Theosophical Publishing House, Adyar.)

27

Section IV. Even the Most Beneficent Practices are Relative

Furthermore, Subhuti, in the practice of charity a Bodhisattva should be detached. That is to say, he should practise charity without regard to appearances; without regard to sound, odour, touch, flavour or any quality. Subhuti, thus should the Bodhisattva practise charity without attachment. Wherefore? In such a case his merit is incalculable.

Subhuti, what do you think? Can you measure all the space extending eastward?

No, World-honoured One, I cannot.

Then can you, Subhuti, measure all the space extending southward, westward, northward, or in any other direction, including nadir and zenith?

No, World-honoured One, I cannot.

Well, Subhuti, equally incalculable is the merit of the Bodhisattva who practises charity without any attachment to appearances. Subhuti, Bodhisattvas should persevere one-pointedly in this instruction.

Note

Compare St. Matthew, Chap. 5, 42, onwards: "Give to him that asketh thee, and from him that would borrow of thee turn not away . . . that ye may be the children of your Father which is in heaven; for he maketh his sun to rise on the evil and the good, and sendeth rain on the just and the unjust."

Love is the highest law. Assistance is an expression of the love of the part for the whole: and courtesy is the splendour of charity.

Section V. Understanding the Ultimate Principle of Reality

Subhuti, what do you think ? Is the Tathagata to be recognized by some material characteristic ?

No, World-honoured One ; the Tathagata cannot be recognized by any material characteristic. Wherefore ? Because the Tathagata has said that material characteristics are not, in fact, material characteristics.

Buddha said: Subhuti, wheresoever are material characteristics there is delusion ; but whoso perceives that all characteristics are in fact no-characteristics, perceives the Tathagata.

Notes

The title of this section gives the clue that it is the kernel of the whole Discourse. It explains all subsequent sections.

"All characteristics are, in fact, no-characteristics." Their source is not in themselves ; they are the proceeds of a Principle.

It might be said that the outset of our quest for Truth is the belief that appearances are illusory, and that realities are to be sought by exploring the Noumenal, not the Phenomenal world. To quote from the Hebrew Scriptures : "Fear of the Lord is the beginning of wisdom."

Section VI. Rare is True Faith

Subhuti said to Buddha : World-honoured One, will there always be men who will truly believe after coming to hear these teachings ?

Buddha answered : Subhuti, do not utter such words ! At the end of the last five-hundred-year period following the passing of the Tathagata, there will be self-controlled men, rooted in merit, coming to hear these teachings, who will be inspired with belief. But you should realize that such men have not strenghtened their root of merit under just one Buddha, or two Buddhas, or three, or four, or five Buddhas, but under countless Buddhas ; and their merit is of every kind. Such men, coming to hear these teachings, will have an immediate uprising of pure faith, Subhuti ; and the Tathagata will recognize them. Yes, He will clearly perceive all these of pure heart, and the magnitude of their moral excellences. Wherefore ? It is because such men will not fall back to cherishing the idea of an ego-entity, a personality, a being, or a separated individuality. They will neither fall back to cherishing the idea of things as having intrinsic qualities, nor even of things as devoid of intrinsic qualities.

Wherefore ? Because if such men allowed their minds to grasp and hold on to anything they would be cherishing the idea of an ego-entity, a personality, a being, or a separated individuality ; and if they grasped and held on to the notion of things as having intrinsic qualities they would be cherishing the idea of an ego-entity, a personality, a being, or a separated individuality. Likewise, if they grasped and held on to the notion of things as devoid of intrinsic qualities they would be cherishing the idea of an ego-entity, a personality, a being, or a separated individuality. So you should not be attached to things as being possessed of, or devoid of, intrinsic qualities.

This is the reason why the Tathagata always teaches this saying : My teaching of the Good Law is to be likened unto a raft. The Buddha-teaching must be relinquished ; how much more so mis-teaching !

Notes

"The last five-hundred-year period"--i.e., 2,500 years after Buddha's passing ; the present era. It is described prophetically as the period of dissension, schisms, and decay of faith.

"Under countless Buddhas" ; consider the previous Section. A succession of Buddhas in time and space is an objective manifestation. All the Buddhas *are* Buddha.

Faith is the Bodhisattva's first qualification for his goal of Perfect Wisdom.

"You should not be attached to things as being possessed of, or devoid of intrinsic qualities" (Lit. : dharma and adharma). Anyone learning to ride a horse is concerned with the hazard of falling off, but the practised rider is neither concerned with falling off, nor concerned with keeping his balance.

The saying of the Raft is quoted from the *Majjhima Nikaya*, 1-134. A question is asked : Does a man who has safely crossed a flood upon a raft continue his journey carrying that raft upon his head ? So long as the mind is attached even to Buddha's teaching, as a basis, it will cherish the idea of "I" and "Other."

Good Law = Dharma.

Bibliography

For the *Majjhima Nikaya* 1-134, see : *Some Sayings of the Buddha*, p. 316, or *Sacred Books of the Buddhists*, Vol. 5. (Pali Text Society.)

Section VII. Great Ones, Perfect Beyond Learning, Utter no Words of Teaching

Subhuti, what do you think ? Has the Tathagata attained the Consummation of Incomparable Enlightenment ? Has the Tathagata a teaching to enunciate ?

Subhuti answered : As I understand Buddha's meaning there is no formulation of truth called Consummation of Incomparable Enlightenment. Moreover, the Tathagata has no formulated teaching to enunciate. Wherefore ? Because the Tathagata has said that truth is uncontainable and inexpressible. It neither *is* nor is it *not*.

Thus it is that this unformulated Principle is the foundation of the different systems of all the sages.

Notes

Truth is not contained by its expressions, nor fathomed by its definitions, nor revealed by its titles.

It *is*, because without it there could be no reality ; it is *not*, because everything which *is* literally implies a limitation. A Principle, in Itself, is unindigent, *not in need of anything ; i.e., having an exempt transcendency by which it is beyond necessity in respect of, and wholly unaffected by anything*, of anything which it issues or ordinates (Lit. : "Not dharma, not adharma").

"Great Ones, Perfect beyond learning" = Ashaiksa.

"Unformulated Principle" = Wu wei fa (where this idiom occurs in Chinese Buddhist Sutras it should not be given the same connotation as in Taoist literature).

Subhuti, what do you think? If anyone filled three thousand galaxies of worlds with the seven treasures and gave all away in gifts of alms, would he gain great merit?

Subhuti said: Great indeed, World-honoured One! Wherefore? Because merit partakes of the character of no-merit, the Tathagata characterized the merit as great.

Then Buddha said: On the other hand, if anyone received and retained even only four lines of this Discourse and taught and explained them to others, his merit would be the greater. Wherefore? Because, Subhuti, from this Discourse issue forth all the Buddhas and the Consummation of Incomparable Enlightenment teachings of all the Buddhas.

Subhuti, what is called "the Religion given by Buddha" is not, in fact, Buddha-Religion.

Notes

"The seven treasures"—Gold, silver, lapis-lazuli, crystal, agate, red pearls, cornelian.

The merit of such charity is objective, so it is characterized by the quality "great," which is relative. Real merit would be beyond qualification.

"Four lines." (Lit.: Four lines, equal to one gatha.)

"Buddha-teachings . . ." Perfect wisdom is not "teaching." Teachings may point to the goal, but do not contain it.

Enlightenment means At-one with Light. Herein is no distinction between perceiver, perceiving and perceived.

Section IX. Real Designation is Undesignate

Subhuti, what do you think ? Does a disciple who has entered the Stream of the Holy Life say within himself: I obtain the fruit of a Stream-entrant ?

Subhuti said : No, World-honoured One. Wherefore ? Because "Stream-entrant" is merely a name. There is no stream-entering. The disciple who pays no regard to form, sound, odour, taste, touch, or any quality, is called a Stream-entrant.

Subhuti, what do you think ? Does an adept who is subject to only one more rebirth say within himself : I obtain the fruit of a Once-to-be-reborn ?

Subhuti said : No, World-honoured One. Wherefore ? Because "Once-to-be-reborn" is merely a name. There is no passing away nor coming into existence. [The adept who realizes]—this is called "Once-to-be-reborn."

Subhuti, what do you think ? Does a venerable one who will never more be reborn as a mortal say within himself : I obtain the fruit of a Non-returner ?

Subhuti said : No, World-honoured One. Wherefore ? Because "Non-returner" is merely a name. There is no non-returning ; hence the designation "Non-returner."

Subhuti, what do you think ? Does a holy one say within himself: I have obtained Perfective Enlightenment ?

Subhuti said : No, World-honoured One. Wherefore ? Because there is no such condition as that called "Perfective Enlightenment." World-honoured One, if a holy one of Perfective Enlightenment said to himself "such am I," he would necessarily partake of the idea of an ego-entity, a personality, a being, or a separated individuality. World-honoured One, when the Buddha declares that I excel amongst holy men in the Yoga of perfect quiescence, in dwelling in seclusion, and in freedom from passions, I do not say within myself : I am a holy one of Perfective Enlightenment, free from passions. World-honoured One, if I said within myself : Such am I ; you would not declare : Subhuti finds happiness abiding in peace, in seclusion in the midst of the forest. This is because Subhuti abides no where : therefore he is called, "Subhuti, Joyful-Abider-in-Peace, Dweller-in-Seclusion-in-the-Forest."

Notes

Claiming spiritual superiority is separative and tends to enhance the illusory personality.

"There is no passing away . . ." The passage in square brackets is included to provide a sense at first reading. Upon meditating, it can be discarded. If all life is One, there is no-one to *realise* it. The Oneness of the totality of all things is the Real ; components have no ultimate intrinsic reality. P.T.O.

"Dweller in seclusion in the forest." There is a double meaning here. Ascetic hermitage, and dwelling aloof and immune from distraction and temptation in the dark forest tangle of human perplexities and desires. Cf. *The Dhammapada*, 20, 283 : "Cut down the whole forest, not just a single tree. . . . Cut down the great trees and clear away the undergrowth; then, Monks, will you be free from the forest." (Root out lust and transmute the whole layer of lustful consciousness.)

"Subhuti abides no where." The hermit's peace is a phenomenal condition, attached to the distinction between "I" and "not-I."

Stream-entrant = Srota-apanna. (This is the first stage of Arhatship and is far advanced beyond Shravaka or Neophyte.)

Adept subject to only one more rebirth = Sakridagamin. (The second stage. Once more only to be reborn as a mortal.)

A venerable one who will never more be reborn as a mortal = Anagamin. (The third stage. He will be reborn in a higher world, or in heaven, and in that existence will attain full Arhatship.)

Holy one of Perfective Enlightenment = Arhat. (The fourth and final stage, not subject to any of the agencies which condition phenomenal existence.)
Joyful-Abider-in-Peace . . . = Aranyaka.

Bibliography

The Dhammapada. F. Max Muller. *Sacred Books of the East.* Vol. 10. Or Edited by J.A. (*The Buddhist Society.*) Also in the *Wisdom of the East Series*, and many other editions.

Section X. Setting Forth Pure Lands

Buddha said : Subhuti, what do you think ?   In the remote past when the Tathagata was with Dipankara Buddha, did he have any degree of attainment in the Good Law ?

No, World-honoured One.   When the Tathagata was with Dipankara Buddha he had no degree of attainment in the Good Law.

Subhuti, what do you think ? Does a Bodhisattva set forth any majestic Buddha-lands ?

No, World-honoured One.   Wherefore ? Because setting forth majestic Buddha-lands is not a majestic setting forth ; this is merely a name.

[Then Buddha continued :] Therefore, Subhuti, all Bodhisattvas, lesser and great, should develop a pure, lucid mind, not depending upon sound, flavour, touch, odour or any quality. A Bodhisattva should develop a mind which alights upon no thing whatsoever ; and so should he establish it.

Subhuti, this may be likened to a human frame as large as the mighty Mount Sumeru. What do you think ?   Would such a body be great ?

Subhuti replied : Great indeed, World-honoured One.   This is because Buddha has explained that no body is called a great body.

Dipankara Buddha was Gautama Buddha's twenty-fourth predecessor. The advent of a Buddha ever recurs to help humanity with a long interval of time between each.

The Bodhisattva who has attained complete Arhatship may become a spiritual king, presiding over a world of beings whom he never ceases to help by expedient means until all are freed and perfected.

"Would such a body be great?" The real Great transcends conditions and qualities. The study of proportional relationships gives no final clue to the essence of the substance of phenomena. Lao Tzu quotes an ancient proverb : ". . . The greatest square has no angles ; the largest vessel is never complete ; the loudest sound can scarcely be heard ; the biggest form cannot be visualised. Tao, while hidden, is nameless."—(*The Tao Te Ching*, Chap. 41, trans. Ch'u Ta-kao, the Buddhist Society, London.)

Bibliography

The Simple Way of Lao Tzu, by the Editors of the *Shrine of Wisdom*, *Sacred Books of the East*, Vol. 39, and others.

Subhuti, if there were as many Ganges rivers as the sand-grains of the Ganges, would the sand-grains of them all be many?

Subhuti said: Many indeed, World-honoured One! Even the Ganges rivers would be innumerable; how much more so would be their sand-grains?

Subhuti, I will declare a truth to you. If a good man or good woman filled three thousand galaxies of worlds with the seven treasures for each sand-grain in all those Ganges rivers, and gave all away in gifts of alms, would he gain great merit?

Subhuti answered: Great indeed, World-honoured One!

Then Buddha declared: Nevertheless, Subhuti, if a good man or good woman studies this Discourse only so far as to receive and retain four lines, and teaches and explains them to others, the consequent merit would be far greater.

Note
The ability to realise and demonstrate Transcendental Truth depends upon the exercise of pure reason (*Nous*). Herein Truth is known through union of the mind with Reality. The application of the power generated by this union to the welfare of beings results in Transcendental Good, or Holy Grace. Its efficacy is beyond comparing with any number of finite and particular material acts of donation.

Section XII.   Veneration of the True Doctrine

Furthermore, Subhuti, you should know that wheresoever this Discourse is proclaimed, by even so little as four lines, that place should be venerated by the whole realms of Gods, Men and Titans, as though it were a Buddha-Shrine.   How much more is this so in the case of one who is able to receive and retain the whole and read and recite it throughout !

Subhuti, you should know that such an one attains the highest and most wonderful truth. Wheresoever this sacred Discourse may be found there should you comport yourself as though in the presence of Buddha and disciples worthy of honour.

Notes

The inherent universal impulse to worship should be directed to aspiration and mystical love for the highest ideal which a symbol represents, not to the symbol as *an oracle* or a *talisman*.

Titans = Asura (giant demon spirits, constantly at war with the gods).

Section XIII. How this Teaching should be Received and Retained

At that time Subhuti addressed Buddha, saying · World-honoured One, by what name should this Discourse be known, and how should we receive and retain it?

Buddha answered: Subhuti, this Discourse should be known as "The Diamond of the Perfection of Transcendental Wisdom"—thus should you receive and retain it. Subhuti, what is the reason herein? According to the Buddha-teaching the Perfection of Transcendental Wisdom is not really such. "Perfection of Transcendental Wisdom" is just the name given to it. Subhuti, what do you think? Has the Tathagata a teaching to enunciate?

Subhuti replied to Buddha: World-honoured One, the Tathagata has nothing to teach.

Subhuti, what do you think? Would there be many molecules in [the composition of] three thousand galaxies of worlds?

Subhuti said: Many, indeed, World-honoured One!

Subhuti, the Tathagata declares that all these molecules are not really such; they are called "molecules." [Furthermore,] the Tathagata declares that a world is not really a world; it is called "a world."

Subhuti, what do you think? May the Tathagata be perceived by the thirty-two physical peculiarities [of an outstanding sage]?

No, World-honoured One, the Tathagata may not be perceived by these thirty-two marks. Wherefore? Because the Tathagata has explained that the thirty-two marks are not really such; they are called "the thirty-two marks."

Subhuti, if on the one hand a good man or a good woman sacrifices as many lives as the sand-grains of the Ganges, and on the other hand anyone receives and retains even only four lines of this Discourse, and teaches and explains them to others, the merit of the latter will be the greater.

Notes

The diamond cuts into all other materials, but cannot be cut into by any of them. When clean and polished it shines resplendent in the tiniest light, even when immersed in water. If *Vajrachedika* is taken in the sense of "Cutter of the Diamond" we might consider the title as *The Discourse on the Penetration of the Impenetrable.*

Prajna means Wisdom of the highest and clearest kind. It is the last of the Six Paramitas which are the Bodhisattvas' ideals of practice. The others are Charity, Righteousness, Forbearing Patience, Energy and Intense Meditation.

Paramita is derived from *parama :* Superlative, Best, Alpha. It is often translated as "Gone over to the other shore," explained by : Having crossed the troublous flood of mortal existences and reached the haven of Nirvana ; but whatever significance attaches to this interpretation must be considered as symbolical.

The thirty-two marks of an outstanding Sage are pre-Buddhistic in origin, derived from the Hindu Scriptures. The items of the list said to be attributes of the person of Gautama Buddha are probably in part symbolical and in part æsthetic ideals. They will be found detailed in the Lakkhana Sutta of the *Digha Nikaya.*

It will be noticed that the paragraphs of this section are not just variants of the theme, but in each case go deeper than similar ones in preceding sections.

Bibliography

The *Digha Nikaya,* translated in *Sacred Books of the Buddhists,* Vol. 4. Pali Text Society.

Section XIV. Perfect Peace Lies in Freedom from Characteristic Distinctions

Upon the occasion of hearing this Discourse Subhuti had an interior realization of its meaning and was moved to tears. Whereupon he addressed Buddha thus : It is a most precious thing, World-honoured One, that you should deliver this supremely profound Discourse. Never have I heard such an exposition since of old my eye of wisdom first opened. World-honoured One, if anyone listens to this Discourse in faith with a pure, lucid mind, he will thereupon conceive an idea of Fundamental Reality. We should know that such an one establishes the most remarkable virtue. World-honoured One, such an idea of Fundamental Reality is not, in fact, a distinctive idea ; therefore the Tathagata teaches : "Idea of Fundamental Reality" is merely a name.

World-honoured One, having listened to this Discourse, I receive and retain it with faith and understanding. This is not difficult for me, but in ages to come—in the last five hundred years, if there be men coming to hear this Discourse who receive and retain it with faith and understanding, they will be persons of most remarkable achievement. Wherefore ? Because they will be free from the idea of an ego-entity, free from the idea of a personality, free from the idea of a being, and free from the idea of a separated individuality. And why ? Because the distinguishing of an ego-entity is erroneous. Likewise the distinguishing of a personality, or a being, or a separated individuality is erroneous. Consequently those who have left behind every phenomenal distinction are called Buddhas all.

Buddha said to Subhuti: Just as you say! If anyone listens to this Discourse and is neither filled with alarm nor awe nor dread, be it known that such an one is of remarkable achievement. Wherefore? Because, Subhuti, the Tathagata teaches that the First Perfection [the Perfection of Charity] is not, in fact, the First Perfection: such is merely a name.

Subhuti, the Tathagata teaches likewise that the Perfection of Patience is not the Perfection of Patience: such is merely a name. Why so? It is shown thus, Subhuti: When the Rajah of Kalinga mutilated my body, I was at that time free from the idea of an ego-entity, a personality, a being, and a separated individuality. Wherefore? Because then when my limbs were cut away piece by piece, had I been bound by the distinctions aforesaid, feelings of anger and hatred would have been aroused within me. Subhuti, I remember that long ago, sometime during my last past five hundred mortal lives, I was an ascetic practising patience. Even then was I free from those distinctions of separated selfhood. Therefore, Subhuti, Bodhisattvas should leave behind all phenomenal distinctions and awaken the thought of the Consummation of Incomparable Enlightenment by not allowing the mind to depend upon notions evoked by the sensible world—by not allowing the mind to depend upon notions evoked by sounds, odours, flavours, touch-contacts or any qualities. The mind should be kept independent of any thoughts which arise within it. If the mind depends upon anything it has no sure haven. This is why Buddha teaches that the mind of a Bodhisattva should not accept the appearances of things as a basis when exercising charity. Subhuti, as Bodhisattvas practise charity for the welfare of all living beings they should do it in this manner. Just as the Tathagata declares that characteristics are not characteristics, so He declares that all living beings are not, in fact, living beings.

Subhuti, the Tathagata is He who declares that which is true; He who declares that which is fundamental; He who declares that which is ultimate. He does not declare that which is deceitful, nor that which is monstrous. Subhuti, that Truth to which the Tathagata has attained is neither real nor unreal.

Subhuti, if a Bodhisattva practises charity with mind attached to formal notions he is like unto a man groping sightless in the gloom; but a Bodhisattva who practises charity with mind detached from any formal notions is like unto a man with open eyes in the radiant glory of the morning, to whom all kinds of objects are clearly visible.

Subhuti, if there be good men and good women in

future ages, able to receive, read and recite this Discourse in its entirety, the Tathagata will clearly perceive and recognise them by means of His Buddha-knowledge; and each one of them will bring immeasurable and incalculable merit to fruition.

Notes

"This is not difficult for me . . ." *The Awakening of Faith*, attributed to the patriarch Ashvaghosha (circa 100 C.E.) says: "When the Tathagata was on earth all men were able to understand Him. His body and mind far excelled those of all other men. When He delivered His perfect words all living beings, though different in kind, understood Him alike." (Dr. T. Richard's translation).

The Rajah of Kalinga was, by legend, a king of Magadha, notorious for violence and cruelty. The incident comes from a story relating how the ladies of his entourage strayed away whilst he slept, and how his insane wrath was aroused when he found them listening attentively to an ascetic, who in a later rebirth became Buddha.

Can the *perfection* of a virtue be claimed unless the mind has transcended the limits of personal self? With such transcendence there is, essentially, no saint to suffer nor fool to be suffered.

The conversion of an ordinary person into a Bodhisattva is marked by three events: (1) He awakens the thought of Enlightenment. (2) He takes vows dedicating himself to the ideal of service for the salvation of all creatures. (3) He receives a prediction from a Buddha of his attainment of the Goal.

"The mind should be kept independent." Thought, in itself, is *positive*. Though it may seem to be inextricably enmeshed with and coloured by sensible perception, this is due to an habitual *laissez faire* reaction to phenomenal stimuli.

The declarations of the Tathagata are concerned with Principal Truth, upon which all relative aspects—including the conformity of thought to things—depends.

"That Truth to which the Tathagata has attained. . . ." The idea of reality implies the idea of unreality, and *vice versa*. As each of these ideas suggests the other they must be linked together in the mind, but by objective comparison they are contradictory. So worldly knowledge is dichotomizing, distinguishing and estimating, but Tathagata-knowledge is formless, imageless, transcendental and free from all dualism.

Ascetic = Rishi. Perfection of Patience = Kshantiparamita. Formal notions = dharma.

Bibliography

The Awakening of Faith, by D. T. Suzuki, Open Court Publishing Co., Chicago, 1900, O.P., and T. Richards, Shanghai, 1918, O.P.

Section XV.   The Incomparable Value of This Teaching

Subhuti, if on the one hand, a good man or a good woman performs in the morning as many charitable acts of self-denial as the sand-grains of the Ganges, and performs as many again in the noonday and as many again in the evening, and continues so doing throughout numberless ages, and, on the other hand, anyone listens to this Discourse with heart of faith and without contention, the latter would be the more blessed. But how can any comparison be made with one who writes it down, receives it, retains it, and explains it to others !

Subhuti, we can summarise the matter by saying that the full value of this Discourse can neither be conceived nor estimated, nor can any limit be set to it.   The Tathagata has declared this teaching for the benefit of initiates of the Great Way ;   he has declared it for the benefit of initiates of the Supreme Way. Whosoever can receive and retain this teaching, study it, recite it and spread it abroad will be clearly perceived and recognized by the Tathagata and will achieve a perfection of merit beyond measurement or calculation—a perfection of merit unlimited and inconceivable.   In every case such an one will exemplify the Tathagata-Consummation of the Incomparable Enlightenment. Wherefore ?   Because, Subhuti, those who find consolation in limited doctrines involving the conception of an ego-entity, a personality, a being, or a separated individuality, are unable to accept, receive, study, recite and openly explain this Discourse.

Subhuti, in every place where this Discourse is to be found the whole realms of Gods, Men and Titans should offer worship ; for you must know that such a place is sanctified like a shrine, and should properly be venerated by all with ceremonial obeisance and circumambulation and with offerings of flowers and incense.

<hr />

Notes

The idea of self-denial implies the idea of self-assertion.

Worshippers pass round Buddhist Shrines, Temples and Monuments on the left-hand side, keeping the sacred object on their right.

Section XVI. Purgation through Suffering the Retribution for Past Sins

Furthermore, Subhuti, if it be that good men and good women, who receive and retain this Discourse, are downtrodden, their evil destiny is the inevitable retributive result of sins committed in their past mortal lives.   By virtue of their present misfortunes the reacting effects of their past will be thereby worked out, and they will be in a position to attain the Consummation of Incomparable Enlightenment.

Subhuti, I remember the infinitely remote past before Dipankara Buddha.   There were 84,000 myriads of multi-millions of Buddhas and to all these I made offerings ; yes, all these I served without the least trace of fault.   Nevertheless, if anyone is able to receive, retain, study, and recite this Discourse at the end of the last [500-year] period he will gain such a merit that mine in the service of all the Buddhas could not be reckoned as one-hundredth part of it, not even one-thousandth part of it, not even one thousand myriad multi-millionth part of it—indeed, no such comparison is possible.

Subhuti, if I fully detailed the merit gained by good men and good women coming to receive, retain, study, and recite this Discourse in the last period, my hearers would be filled with doubt and might become disordered in mind, suspicious and unbelieving.   You should know, Subhuti, that the significance of this Discourse is beyond conception; likewise the fruit of its rewards is beyond conception.

"The significance of this Discourse. . . ." The extent and value of its meaning and importance cannot be materially gauged.

Furthermore its meaning must be *realized* because it cannot be understood without direct experience.

The same may also be said of the significance of "Tathagata" which in Chinese is composed of two characters, the first meaning So, thus (and is also used in the sense of : Suchness, absolute reality), and the second meaning Come.

Section XVII. No One Attains Transcendental Wisdom

At that time Subhuti addressed Buddha, saying : World-honoured One, if good men and good women seek the Consummation of Incomparable Enlightenment, by what criteria should they abide and how should they control their thoughts ?

Buddha replied to Subhuti : Good men and good women seeking the Consummation of Incomparable Enlightenment must create this resolved attitude of mind : I must liberate all living beings, yet when all have been liberated, verily not any one is liberated. Wherefore ? If a Bodhisattva cherishes the idea of an ego-entity, a personality, a being, or a separated individuality, he is consequently *not* a Bodhisattva, Subhuti. This is because in reality there is no formula which gives rise to the Consummation of Incomparable Enlightenment.

Subhuti, what do you think ? When the Tathagata was with Dipankara Buddha was there any formula for the attainment of the Consummation of Incomparable Enlightenment ?

No, World-honoured One, as I understand Buddha's meaning, there was no formula by which the Tathagata attained the Consummation of Incomparable Enlightenment.

Buddha said : You are right, Subhuti ! Verily there was no formula by which the Tathagata attained the Consummation of Incomparable Enlightenment. Subhuti, had there been any such formula, Dipankara Buddha would not have predicted concerning me : "In the ages of the future you will come to be a Buddha called Shakyamuni" ; but Dipankara Buddha made that prediction concerning me because there is actually no formula for the attainment of the Consummation of Incomparable Enlightenment. The reason herein is that Tathagata is a signification implying all formulas. In case anyone says that the Tathagata attained the Consummation of Incomparable Enlightenment, I tell you truly, Subhuti, that there is no formula by which the Buddha attained it. Subhuti, the basis of Tathagata's attainment of the Consummation of Incomparable Enlightenment is wholly *beyond* ; it is neither real nor unreal. Hence I say that the whole realm of formulations is not really such, therefore it is called "Realm of formulations."

Subhuti, a comparison may be made with [the idea of] a gigantic human frame.

Then Subhuti said : The World-honoured One has declared that such is not a great body ; "a great body" is just the name given to it.

Subhuti, it is the same concerning Bodhisattvas. If a Bodhisattva announces : I will liberate all living creatures, he is not rightly called a Bodhisattva. Wherefore ? Because, Subhuti, there is really no such condition as that called Bodhisattvaship, because Buddha teaches that all things are devoid of selfhood, devoid of personality, devoid of entity, and devoid of separate individuality. Subhuti, if a

Bodhisattva announces : I will set forth majestic Buddha-lands one does not call him a Bodhisattva, because the Tathagata has declared that the setting forth of majestic Buddha-lands is not really such : "a majestic setting forth" is just the name given to it.

Subhuti, Bodhisattvas who are wholly devoid of any conception of separate selfhood are truthfully called Bodhisattvas.

Notes

"Shakyamuni" is a title of the Buddha meaning : Holy Sage of the Shakya Clan.

In the eighth of the ten stages of the spiritual progress of a Bodhisattva, he is established beyond all falling back, and a prediction (*vyakarana*) of his attainment of the goal is made to him by a Buddha. Upon the occasion of the prediction referred to, our Buddha—then a Bodhisattva—offered five lotus flowers to Dipankara Buddha.

For an account of Gautama Buddha's prediction concerning Subhuti, and others, see the Lotus Sutra chaps. 6, 8 and 9.

For assistance with this part it is useful to reflect upon the question : Why predict the predictable ?

In the 8th century C.E., the 33rd Mahayana patriarch, the Venerable Hui Neng (or Wei Lang) related in his autobiography that he first contacted Buddhism through hearing a street-recital of this Discourse, and later became thoroughly enlightened during a sermon upon Section X.

In one of his own sermons Hui Neng said : "Why should we formulate any system of Law when our goal can be reached no matter whether we turn to the right or to the left ? Since it is with our own efforts that we realize the essence of mind, and since the realization and the practice of the Law are both done instantaneously and not gradually or stage by stage, the formulation of any system of Law is therefore unnecessary. As all Dharmas are intrinsically Nirvanic, how can there be gradation in them ?" (Wong Mou-lam's translation, chap. 8).

". . . Wholly *beyond*; neither real nor unreal." The Norm, or the Mean, entirely outside the scope of dualistic opposites and co-relatives.

Formula = dharma. Whole realm of Formulations = sarvadharma.

Bibliography

For the Lotus Sutra (*Saddharmapundarika*) see : *Sacred Books of the East*, Vol. 21, by H. Kern. (Clarendon Press). *The Lotus of The Wonderful Law* by W. Soothill. (Oxford University Press).

For the teachings of Hui Neng, see : *The Sutra of Wei Lang* by Wong Mou-lam. (Buddhist Society, 1945.)

Section XVIII. *All Modes of mind are Really Only Mind*

Subhuti, what do you think ? Does the Tathagata possess the human eye ?

Yes, World-honoured One, He does.

Well, do you think the Tathagata possesses the divine eye ?

Yes, World-honoured One, He does.

And do you think the Tathagata possesses the gnostic eye ?

Yes, World-honoured One, He does.

And do you think the Tathagata possesses the eye of transcendent wisdom ?

Yes, World-honoured One, He does.

And do you think the Tathagata possesses the Buddha-eye of omniscience ?

Yes, World-honoured One, He does.

Subhuti, what do you think ? Concerning the sand-grains of the Ganges, has the Buddha taught about them ?

Yes, World-honoured One, the Tathagata has taught concerning these grains.

Well, Subhuti, if there were as many Ganges rivers as the sand-grains of the Ganges and there was a Buddha-land for each sand-grain in all those Ganges rivers, would those Buddha-lands be many ?

[Subhuti replied] : Many indeed, World-honoured One !

Then Buddha said : Subhuti, however many living beings there are in all those Buddha lands, though they have manifold modes of mind, the Tathagata understands them all. Wherefore ? Because the Tathagata teaches that all these are not Mind ; they are merely called "mind." Subhuti, it is impossible to retain past mind, impossible to hold on to present mind, and impossible to grasp future mind.

Section XIX. *Absolute Reality is the Only Foundation*

Subhuti, what do you think? If anyone filled three thousand galaxies of worlds with the seven treasures and gave all away in gifts of alms, would he gain great merit?

Yes, indeed, World-honoured One, he would gain great merit!

Subhuti, if such merit was Real, the Tathagata would not have declared it to be great, but because it is without a foundation the Tathagata characterised it as "great."

Section XX. The Unreality of Phenomenal Distinctions

Subhuti, what do you think ? Can the Buddha be perceived by His perfectly-formed body ?

No, World-honoured One, the Tathagata cannot be perceived by His perfectly-formed body, because the Tathagata teaches that a perfectly-formed body is not really such ; it is merely called "a perfectly-formed body."

Subhuti, what do you think ? Can the Tathagata be perceived by means of any phenomenal characteristic ?

No, World-honoured One, the Tathagata may not be perceived by any phenomenal characteristic, because the Tathagata teaches that phenomenal characteristics are not really such ; they are merely termed "phenomenal characteristics."

Section XXI. Words cannot express Truth. That which Words Express is not Truth

Subhuti, do not say that the Tathagata conceives the idea : I must set forth a Teaching. For if anyone says that the Tathagata sets forth a Teaching he really slanders Buddha and is unable to explain what I teach. As to any Truth-declaring system, Truth is undeclarable ; so "an enunciation of Truth" is just the name given to it.

Thereupon, Subhuti spoke these words to Buddha: World-honoured One, in the ages of the future will there be men coming to hear a declaration of this Teaching who will be inspired with belief ?

And Buddha answered : Subhuti, those to whom you refer are neither living beings nor not-living beings. Wherefore ? Because "living beings," Subhuti, these "living beings" are not really such ; they are just called by that name.

Section XXII. *It Cannot be Said that Anything is Attainable*

'Then Subhuti asked Buddha: World-honoured One, in the attainment of the Consummation of Incomparable Enlightenment did Buddha make no acquisition whatsoever?

Buddha replied: Just so, Subhuti. Through the Consummation of Incomparable Enlightenment I acquired not even the least thing; wherefore it is called "Consummation of Incomparable Enlightenment."

Note
It is the *Consummation* of Incomparable Enlightenment.

Section XXIII. *The Practice of Good Works Purifies the Mind*

Furthermore, Subhuti, *This* is altogether everywhere, without differentiation or degree ; wherefore it is called "Consummation of Incomparable Enlightenment."   It is straightly attained by freedom from separate personal selfhood and by cultivating all kinds of goodness.

Subhuti, though we speak of "goodness" the Tathagata declares that there is no goodness ; such is merely a name.

Notes

"Altogether everywhere . . ."   Samata.   Universal sameness ; having no partiality.   It is the Consummation of *Incomparable* Enlightenment.

We say that good and evil *exist*, but to assert the *being* of Good would imply the *being* of Evil.   Evil is negative and merely *ex-ists* in so far as Reality is seen from the point of view of diverse particularity.

Section XXIV. *The Incomparable Merit of This Teaching*

Subhuti, if there be one who gives away in gifts of alms a mass of the seven treasures equal in extent to as many mighty Mount Sumerus as there would be in three thousand galaxies of worlds, and if there be another who selects even only four lines from this Discourse upon the Perfection of Transcendental Wisdom, receiving and retaining them, and clearly expounding them to others, the merit of the latter will be so far greater than that of the former that no conceivable comparison can be made between them.

Section XXV. The Illusion of Ego

Subhuti, what do you think? Let no one say the Tathagata cherishes the idea: I must liberate all living beings. Allow no such thought, Subhuti. Wherefore? Because in reality there are no living beings to be liberated by the Tathagata. If there were living beings for the Tathagata to liberate, He would partake in the idea of selfhood, personality entity, and separate individuality.

Subhuti, though the common people accept egoity as real, the Tathagata declares that ego is not different from non-ego. Subhuti, whom the Tathagata referred to as "common people" are not really common people; such is merely a name.

Section XXVI. *The Body of Truth has no Marks*

Subhuti, what do you think? May the Tathagata be perceived by the thirty-two marks [of a great man]?

Subhuti answered: Yes, certainly the Tathagata may be perceived thereby.

Then Buddha said: Subhuti, if the Tathagata may be perceived by such marks any great imperial ruler is the same as the Tathagata.

Subhuti then said to Buddha: World-honoured One, as I understand the meaning of Buddha's words the Tathagata may not be perceived by the thirty-two marks.

Whereupon the World-honoured One uttered this verse:

Who sees Me by form,
Who seeks Me in sound,
Perverted are his footsteps upon the Way;
For he cannot perceive the Tathagata.

Notes

Subhuti's departure may be due to a defect in the Chinese translation. Although the Chinese commentators refer to a lapse on the part of the venerable disciple, in the Sanskrit version he gives the expected reply in the negative.   P.T.O.

At the birth of the baby prince who grew up to be Gautama Buddha, the marks were observed and it was foretold that He would become either a king whose chariot-wheels would roll everywhere, or a pre-eminent sage who would set a-rolling the wheel of the Good Law throughout the world. Of these alternatives, King Sudhodana yearned for his son to be the material conqueror.

Great imperial ruler = Chakravarti.

Bibliography

See : The Buddhacharita. *Sacred Books of the East*, vol. 49, and the *Light of Asia*. Sir Edwin Arnold.

Section XXVII. It is Erroneous to Affirm that All Things are Ever Extinguished

Subhuti, if you should conceive the idea that the Tathagata attained the Consummation of Incomparable Enlightenment by reason of His perfect form, do not countenance such thoughts. The Tathagata's attainment was not by reason of His perfect form.   [On the other hand] Subhuti, if you should conceive the idea that anyone in whom dawns the Consummation of Incomparable Enlightenment declares that all manifest standards are ended and extinguished, do not countenance such thoughts.   Wherefore ?   Because the man in whom the Consummation of Incomparable Enlightenment dawns does not affirm concerning any formula that it is finally extinguished.

The perfect body and deportment of the Buddha is an appearance of His wisdom and compassion.

In terms of Western Philosophy, the basis of all laws, standards, duties and regulations is Order, which is the proceeding of *The Good*. We may compare the *Lankavatara Sutra*, Chap. 2, XVIII : "Further, Mahamati, those who, afraid of sufferings arising from the discrimination of birth and death, seek for Nirvana, do not know that birth-and-death and Nirvana are not to be separated the one from the other; and seeing that all things subject to discrimination have no reality, imagine that Nirvana consists in the future annihilation of the senses and their fields."

All manifest standards = Sarvadharma.   Formula = dharma.

Bibliography

The Diamond Sutra. By W. Gemmell. (Kegan Paul Trench Trubner and Co., Ltd., O.P.).

The Lankavatara Sutra. By D. T. Suzuki. (Routledge, London, 1932).

Section XXVIII. *Attachment to Rewards of Merit*

Subhuti, if one Bodhisattva bestows in charity sufficient of the seven treasures to fill as many worlds as there be sand-grains in the river Ganges, and another, realizing that all things are egoless, attains perfection through patient forbearance, the merit of the latter will far exceed that of the former. Why is this, Subhuti ?   It is because all Bodhisattvas are insentient as to the rewards of merit.

Then Subhuti said to Buddha : What is this saying, World-honoured One, that Bodhisattvas are insentient as to rewards of merit ?

[And Buddha answered] : Subhuti, Bodhisattvas who achieve merit should not be fettered with desire for rewards.   Thus it is said that the rewards of merit are not received.

Notes
Compare the Hindu *Bhagavad Gita*, Book II, 46 and 47.   "Thy right is to the work, but never to its fruits ; let not the fruit of thy work be thy motive, nor take refuge in abstinence from works. Standing in union with the Soul, carry out thy work, putting away attachment, O conqueror of wealth ; equal in success and failure, for equalness is called union with the Soul."   (Johnston's translation.)

Bibliography
The Bhagavad Gita. By Charles Johnston.   (Quarterly Book Department, New York, 1908.)
The Lay of the Adorable One.   By Annie Besant.   (Theosophical Publishing House), London, and many others.

Section XXIX. Perfect Tranquility

Subhuti, if anyone should say that the Tathagata comes or goes or sits or reclines, he fails to understand my teaching Why ? Because TATHAGATA has neither whence nor whither, therefore is He called "Tathagata."

Notes

For assistance with this vital passage it will be found useful to study the 5th and 6th chapters of the *Lankavatara Sutra*.

Section XXX. The Integral Principle

Subhuti, if a good man or a good woman ground an infinite number of galaxies of worlds to dust, would the resulting minute particles be many ?

Subhuti replied : Many indeed, World-honoured One ! Wherefore ? Because if such were really minute particles Buddha would not have spoken of them as minute particles. For as to this, Buddha has declared that they are not really such. "Minute particles" is just the name given to them. Also, World-honoured One, when the Tathagata speaks of galaxies of worlds these are not worlds ; for if reality could be predicated of a world it would be a self-existent cosmos and the Tathagata teaches that there is really no such thing. "Cosmos" is merely a figure of speech.

[Then Buddha said] : Subhuti, words cannot explain the real nature of a cosmos. Only common people fettered with desire make use of this arbitrary method.

Notes
The riddle of existence cannot be elucidated by objective reasoning, which is essentially conventional (*Samvriti-satya* or *Vyavahara*). As is said in the *Lotus Sutra* (Chap. 15), "For the Tathagata sees the triple world as it really is : it is not born, it dies not ; it is not conceived, it springs not into existence ; it moves not in a whirl, it becomes not extinct ; it is not real, nor unreal ; it is not existing, nor non-existing ; it is not such, not

otherwise, nor false. The Tathagata sees . . . not as the ignorant common people . . . in his position no laws are concealed. (Dr. Kern's translation.)

Sages of all times and lands have realised that any fixed proposition which may be asserted as to the real nature of the universe can be refuted by dialectic.

Bibliography

Saddharmapundarika. By H. Kern. (Sacred Books of the East, Vol. 21.)

The Lotus of the Wonderful Law. By W. E. Soothill. (Clarendon Press, 1930.) (Chap. 16 of the text used by Dr. Soothill translates the above passage.)

Section XXXI. *Conventional Truth Should be Cut Off*

Subhuti, if anyone should say that Buddha declares any conception of egoity do you consider he would understand my teaching aright?

No, World-honoured One, such a man would not have any sound understanding of the Tathagata's teaching, because the World-honoured One declares that notions of selfhood, personality, entity and separate individuality, as really existing, are erroneous—these terms are merely figures of speech.

[Thereupon Buddha said]: Subhuti, those who aspire to the Consummation of Incomparable Enlightenment should recognize and understand all varieties of things in the same way and cut off the arising of [views which are mere] aspects. Subhuti, as regards aspects, the Tathagata declares that in reality they are not such. They are called "aspects."

Subhuti, someone might fill innumerable worlds with the seven treasures and give all away in gifts of alms, but if any good man or any good woman awakens the thought of Enlightenment and takes even only four lines from this Discourse, reciting, using, receiving, retaining and spreading them abroad and explaining them for the benefit of others, it will be far more meritorious.

Now in what manner may he explain them to others ? By detachment from appearances—abiding in Real Truth.—So I tell you—

Thus shall ye think of all this fleeting world :

A star at dawn, a bubble in a stream ;

A flash of lightning in a summer cloud,

A flickering lamp, a phantom, and a dream.*

When Buddha finished this Discourse the venerable Subhuti, together with the bhikshus, bhikshunis, lay-brothers and sisters, and the whole realms of Gods, Men and Titans, were filled with joy by His teaching, and, taking it sincerely to heart they went their ways.

Notes

*This charming verse is Dr. Kenneth Saunders' translation of the gatha.

Ultimate Truth is Absolute Reality. In this Principle all things are one, and their individuality and diversity depend upon mutual reference. Looking at this statement from our habitual point of view we see that it implies the idea : Within every man and woman is the Buddha-seed.

To awaken the thought of enlightenment is to begin to penetrate the mists and veils of mutually interdependent created things in our search for union with That which is beyond all names, commotions, characteristics, qualities, appearances and concepts.

A Bhikshuni is a nun of the Order.

Bibliography

The verse is quoted from *Lotuses of the Mahayana*. By K. Saunders (Wisdom of the East Series).

Book Two

The Sutra of Hui Neng

CONTENTS

The seventh century gave birth to a new phase of Buddhism called Ch'an. The centuries since that time have adulterated and specialized this teaching. In the present time, here in America, it is known as Zen.

The man through whom Ch'an came into this world was Hui Neng. He later received the honor of being named the Sixth Patriarch.

This Sutra contains the essence not only of Buddhism but of all Great Religions. The Sutra extends to you, the reader, the possibility of coming to the full realization of Enlightenment; in, of, and through your own understanding. You need not turn to any ritual, dogma, or creed; just keep reading it. The only worthwhile practice is to understand.

When you have reached understanding, you will realize the Light never seen on land or sea. You will not have to do, or strain for gain; you will know Who you Are; then you will only have to Be. This, my friend, is the Key to Eternity.

May I draw your attention to the fact that only mind is mentioned and not heart in the translation of the Sutra. The reason is that the Chinese character meaning mind and heart, is the same. The translator made it mind throughout this version. Each time mind essence is referred to (in the opinion of this writer) it means heart-mind (even as the esoteric meaning of the Yab-Yum imagery of Tibet). Keep this in your consciousness as you read the Sutra. Learn to feel-think from the depths of Being. Discard sentimentality; feel the real. Know that all which our senses contact is but a limited expression of unity in diversity. Know that beyond objectivity and subjectivity is That which you Are. When you can experience this, you realize the Essence. Then intuitive spontaneity is functional for you.

If you can let this Sutra happen for you, you will enjoy "unendurable pleasure indefinitely prolonged."

FALL AWAKE, my friend!

May all beings be well,

May all beings be happy.

Joe Miller

FOREWORD TO EDITION OF 1953

THE first, and apparently the only published translation into English of the *Sutra of Wei Lang* (Hui Neng) was completed by the late Mr. Wong Mou-lam in 1930, and published in the form of a 4to paper-covered book by the Yu Ching Press of Shanghai. Copies were imported to London a few dozen at a time by the Buddhist Society, London, until 1939, when the remaining stock was brought to England and soon sold out. The demand, however, has persisted ; hence this new edition.

Three courses were open to the present publishers; to republish the translation as it stood, with all its imperfections, to prepare an entirely new translation, with commentary, or to 'polish up' the existing version without in any way altering the sense. As the first seemed undesirable, and the second impracticable at the present time, the third course was adopted.

As Mr. Wong Mou-lam died in 1936, to the great loss of Western scholarship, it has been impossible to invoke his approval of the revisions made in his text. I have therefore scrupulously avoided any re-writing or even paraphrasing, and knowing how many users of the Sutra had learnt whole passages of its somewhat quaint phraseology by heart, I have confined myself to the minimum of alterations.

A few words were so obviously incorrect, due to the translator's imperfect knowledge of English. that I have substituted others which I am sure he would have approved. I have improved the punctuation, sequence of tenses, and certain awkward or clumsy phrasing, in the course of which I noted how the translator's grasp of English improved as the work went on.

It will be noticed how Mr. Wong Mou-lam assisted his readers to grasp the meaning of certain key terms, such as Prajna, Samadhi and Dhyana, without offering any single English term as a final equivalent. Sometimes he gives the Sanskrit word with one English meaning after it in brackets ; later he gives a different English word with the Sanskrit term in brackets after it. Thus the meaning of the word is

5

built up in the reader's mind in part at least of its manifold complexity. Later in the work he tends to leave the word untranslated, as though satisfied that the student had learnt what it meant in the original. It may be helpful to remind readers that the Sanskrit term, Dhyana, was corrupted in China into Ch'an, and in Japan into Zen.*

On the rare occasions on which the actual meaning of a passage was in doubt I have compared it with the late Mr. Dwight Goddard's version, which first appeared in *A Buddhist Bible*, published by him at Thetford, Vermont, U.S.A., in 1932. I have found this edition of occasional assistance, and have incorporated Mr. Goddard's valuable note on page 99.

I have somewhat shortened the original Preface of Mr. Dih Ping Tsze, the translator's patron and inspirer, but left in most of his valuable footnotes.

For the rest, this unique work, 'the only Sutra spoken by a native of China,' may be left to speak for itself in the form in which Mr. Wong Mou-lam gave it us. May it play its part in guiding Western thought and action into the Middle Way which leads to peace and to the heart's enlightenment.

CHRISTMAS HUMPHREYS.

December 1952.

---

* But Dr. D. T. Suzuki has since pointed out (The Eastern Buddhist, New Series, Vol. I No. 1 pp. 123-4) that in the process of transliteration the term *ch'an* was adopted by the Chinese for a phonetic reason, " and 'Zen' has in it none of the meanings of the Sanskrit word. . . The unique position held by Hui Neng in Zen history is due chiefly to his insistence that there be the awakening in *prajna* (transcendental wisdom) rather than mere absorption in quiet sitting (*dhyana*)." (Ed. 1966).

6

EDITOR'S FOREWORD TO FOURTH EDITION

THE history of English Translations of this famous Sutra appears in the Foreword to the edition of 1953 included herein. To bring this up to date I must add the translation by Charles Luk which is included in *Ch'an and Zen Teaching*, Series Three, published by Rider in 1962, and that by Wing Tsit-Chan published as *The Platform Sutra* by St. John's University Press, New York, in 1963. This latter is based on the much earlier Tun-huang MS which came to light in 1900. Some lovers of this basic text of Ch'an Buddhism take the view that these later translations provide for the practising Zen student little substantial improvement on the pioneer effort of Wong Mou-lam, and have the disadvantage of appearing in larger and more expensive form. It is in the belief that the Sutra should still be available in pocket form, and at a minimum price, that the Buddhist Society has produced this new edition.

We are most grateful to Luzac and Co., who for some years have published and marketed the Wong Mou-lam edition for the Society. In relinquishing their rights they have enabled the Society itself to resume control of a work which it was the first to bring to the West just thirty-five years ago.

But the time had come to substitute for the names as given by Wong Mou-lam the form of them now generally adopted by Western scholars. Thus the name of the author himself, long given as Wei-lang, becomes Hui Neng, and the monastery at which the Sutra was delivered is changed from Pao Lam to Pao Lin.

For these numerous changes I am grateful to Mr. Charles Luk, of Hongkong, and Dr. Richard Chi, late of Oxford University. For the preparation of the text with such new renderings, and helpful suggestions for further minor improvements, I am grateful to Mr. Gerald Yorke, who has done so much to bring the work of Mr. Charles Luk before the English-speaking public.

CHRISTMAS HUMPHREYS.

London, 1966.

PREFACE

It has long been my desire to have this Sutra translated into a European language so that the Message of Zen may be transmitted to the West. The idea obsessed me unremittingly for nearly thirty years, as I could not find a translator to undertake the work until I met Mr. Wong last spring. In an ecstacy of joy, I invited him to stay in my house to translate this Sutra into English. Working on and off, it took him nearly a year and a half to complete the translation. My desire is now fulfilled, and may it prove to be one of the happiest events during the period of the past twelve hundred years.

Now, since an attempt has been made to disseminate this Good Law to the West, I look forward to the day when Europe and America will produce a type of Zen follower whose quick understanding and spontaneous realisation in the solution of the 'Ultimate Problem' will be far superior to our Eastern brethren. Thinking that I have connected the most favourable link with the Occidentals, my happiness is beyond measure.

DIH PING TSZE.

Shanghai, *March 1930*.

TRANSLATOR'S PREFACE

THIS is an English translation of the *Sutra Spoken by the Sixth Patriarch on the High Seat of the Treasure of the Law* (Nanjio's Catalogue No. 1525) which records the sermons and sayings of Hui Neng (638-713), the most famous Dhyana Master of the Tang Dynasty. It may be of interest to note that of all the Chinese works which have been canonized in the Tripitaka, this standard work of the Dhyana School is the only one that bears the designation of 'Sutra,' a designation which is reserved for the sermons of Lord Buddha and those of great Bodhisattvas. Hence it is not without justification to call it 'the only Sutra spoken by a native of China.'

As it takes a poet to translate Virgil, the translator keenly realises how incompetent he is in tackling this difficult task, since neither his knowledge of Buddhism nor his linguistic attainment qualifies him for the work. He reluctantly agreed, however, to bring out an English version of this Sutra, when urged to do so by his teacher, who admits the incompetence of his pupil but still insists that the translation should be done for the following reasons :

(1) That in training himself as a translator for Buddhist work in future, this is a good exercise.

(2) That the translation may receive the benefit of correction and revision from the hands of those who have better qualifications, but not enough time to do the complete work themselves.

(3) That, with due allowance for mistranslation, the book may still be useful to those who cannot read the original, but who had mastered it so well in their previous lives that they only need a paragraph or two, nay even a word or two, to refresh their memory in order to bring back the valuable knowledge that they have now forgotten.

On this understanding alone the translator undertakes the work, and the result of his feeble attempt is now put before the public for what it is worth. As the book stands, the translator knows to his sorrow that the greater part of it will be jargon to readers who have had no previous knowledge of the Dhyana School. May the day come soon when either the translator himself or some other full-fledged Dhyana Master will bring out a new translation with copious notes and explanations, so that the Sutra may be readable by all.

It is from Dr. Ting Fo Po's edition that this translation is made. To this learned gentleman, whose commentaries the translator has made free use of, and to other friends who have given him valuable advice and liberal support he wishes to express his deepest gratitude.

"PUPIL-TRANSLATOR."

(WONG MOU-LAM).

Shanghai, *21st November 1929.*

SUTRA SPOKEN BY THE SIXTH PATRIARCH ON THE HIGH SEAT OF "THE TREASURE OF THE LAW"

CHAPTER I

AUTOBIOGRAPHY

ONCE, when the Patriarch had arrived at Pao Lin Monastery, Prefect Wei of Shao Chou and other officials went there to ask him to deliver public lectures on Buddhism in the hall of Ta Fan Temple in the City (of Canton).

In due course, there were assembled (in the lecture hall) Prefect Wei, government officials and Confucian scholars, about thirty each, and bhikkhus, bhikkhunis, Taoists and laymen to the number of about one thousand. After the Patriarch had taken his seat, the congregation in a body paid him homage and asked him to preach on the fundamental laws of Buddhism. Whereupon, His Holiness delivered the following address :

Learned Audience, our Essence of Mind (literally, self-nature) which is the seed or kernel of enlightenment (Bodhi) is pure by nature, and by making use of this mind alone we can reach Buddhahood directly. Now let me tell you something about my own life and how I came into possession of the esoteric teaching of the Dhyana (or the Zen) School.

My father, a native of Fan Yang, was dismissed from his official post and banished to be a commoner in Hsin Chou in Kwangtung. I was unlucky in that my father died when I was very young, leaving my mother poor and miserable. We moved to Kwang Chou (Canton) and were then in very bad circumstances.

I was selling firewood in the market one day, when one of my customers ordered some to be brought to his shop.

Upon delivery being made and payment received, I left the shop, outside of which I found a man reciting a sutra. As soon as I heard the text of this sutra my mind at once became enlightened. Thereupon I asked the man the name of the book he was reciting and was told that it was the Diamond Sutra (Vajracchedika or Diamond Cutter). I further enquired whence he came and why he recited this particular sutra. He replied that he came from Tung Ch'an Monastery in the Huang Mei District of Ch'i Chou ; that the Abbot in charge of this temple was Hung Yen, the Fifth Patriarch ; that there were about one thousand disciples under him ; and that when he went there to pay homage to the Patriarch, he attended lectures on this sutra. He further told me that His Holiness used to encourage the laity as well as the monks to recite this scripture, as by doing so they might realise their own Essence of Mind, and thereby reach Buddhahood directly.

It must be due to my good karma in past lives that I heard about this, and that I was given ten taels for the maintenance of my mother by a man who advised me to go to Huang Mei to interview the Fifth Patriarch. After arrangements had been made for her, I left for Huang Mei, which took me less than thirty days to reach.

I then went to pay homage to the Patriarch, and was asked where I came from and what I expected to get from him. I replied, "I am a commoner from Hsin Chou of Kwangtung. I have travelled far to pay you respect and I ask for nothing but Buddhahood." "You are a native of Kwangtung, a barbarian ? How can you expect to be a Buddha ?" asked the Patriarch. I replied, "Although there are northern men and southern men, north and south make no difference to their Buddha-nature. A barbarian is different from Your Holiness physically, but there is no difference in our Buddha-nature." He was going to speak further to me, but the presence of other disciples made him stop short. He then ordered me to join the crowd to work.

"May I tell Your Holiness," said I, "that Prajna (transcendental Wisdom) often rises in my mind. When one does not go astray from one's own Essence of Mind, one may be called the 'field of merits.'* I do not know what work Your Holiness would ask me to do."

"This barbarian is too bright," he remarked. "Go to the stable and speak no more." I then withdrew myself to the backyard and was told by a lay brother to split firewood and to pound rice.

More than eight months after, the Patriarch saw me one day and said, "I know your knowledge of Buddhism is very sound, but I have to refrain from speaking to you lest evil doers should do you harm. Do you understand?" "Yes, Sir, I do," I replied. "To avoid people taking notice of me, I dare not go near your hall."

The Patriarch one day assembled all his disciples and said to them, "The question of incessant rebirth is a momentous one. Day after day, instead of trying to free yourselves from this bitter sea of life and death, you seem to go after tainted merits only (*i.e.*, merits which will cause rebirth). Yet merits will be of no help, if your Essence of Mind is obscured. Go and seek for Prajna (wisdom) in your own mind and then write me a stanza (*gatha*) about it. He who understands what the Essence of Mind is will be given the robe (the insignia of the Patriarchate) and the Dharma (*i.e.*, the esoteric teaching of the Dhyana School), and I shall make him the Sixth Patriarch. Go away quickly. Delay not in writing the stanza, as deliberation is quite unnecessary and of no use. The man who has realised the Essence of Mind can speak of it at once, as soon as he is spoken to about it ; and he cannot lose sight of it, even when engaged in battle."

Having received this instruction, the disciples withdrew and said to one another, "It is of no use for us to concentrate our mind to write the stanza and submit it to His Holiness,

---

* A title of honour given to monks, as they afford the best opportunities to others to sow the 'seed' of merits.

13

since the Patriarchate is bound to be won by Shen Hsiu, our instructor. And if we write perfunctorily, it will only be a waste of energy." Upon hearing this, all of them made up their minds not to write and said, "Why should we take the trouble ? Hereafter, we will simply follow our instructor, Shen Hsiu, wherever he goes, and look to him for guidance."

Meanwhile, Shen Hsiu reasoned thus with himself. "Considering that I am their teacher, none of them will take part in the competition. I wonder whether I should write a stanza and submit it to His Holiness. If I do not, how can the Patriarch know how deep or superficial my knowledge is ? If my object is to get the Dharma, my motive is a pure one. If I were after the Patriarchate, then it would be bad. In that case, my mind would be that of a worldling and my action would amount to robbing the Patriarch's holy seat. But if I do not submit the stanza, I shall never have a chance of getting the Dharma. A very difficult point to decide, indeed !"

In front of the Patriarch's hall there were three corridors, the walls of which were to be painted by a court artist, named Lu Chen, with pictures from the Lankavatara (Sutra) depicting the transfiguration of the assembly, and with scenes showing the genealogy of the five Patriarchs for the information and veneration of the public.

When Shen Hsiu had composed his stanza he made several attempts to submit it to the Patriarch, but as soon as he went near the hall his mind was so perturbed that he sweated all over. He could not screw up courage to submit it, although in the course of four days he made altogether thirteen attempts to do so.

Then he suggested to himself, "It would be better for me to write it on the wall of the corridor and let the Patriarch see it for himself. If he approves it, I shall come out to pay homage, and tell him that it is done by me ; but if he disapproves it, then I shall have wasted several years in this mountain in receiving homage from others which I by no means deserve ! In that case, what progress have I made in learning Buddhism ?"

At 12 o'clock that night he went secretly with a lamp to write the stanza on the wall of the south corridor, so that the Patriarch might know what spiritual insight he had attained. The stanza read :

> Our body is the Bodhi-tree,
> And our mind a mirror bright.
> Carefully we wipe them hour by hour,
> And let no dust alight.

As soon as he had written it he left at once for his room; so nobody knew what he had done. In his room he again pondered : "When the Patriarch sees my stanza tomorrow and is pleased with it, I shall be ready for the Dharma; but if he says that it is badly done, it will mean that I am unfit for the Dharma, owing to the misdeeds in previous lives which thickly becloud my mind. It is difficult to know what the Patriarch will say about it !" In this vein he kept on thinking until dawn, as he could neither sleep nor sit at ease.

But the Patriarch knew already that Shen Hsiu had not entered the door of enlightenment, and that he had not known the Essence of Mind.

In the morning, he sent for Mr. Lu, the court artist, and went with him to the south corridor to have the walls there painted with pictures. By chance, he saw the stanza. "I am sorry to have troubled you to come so far," he said to the artist. "The walls need not be painted now, as the Sutra says, 'All forms or phenomena are transient and illusive.' It will be better to leave the stanza here, so that people may study it and recite it. If they put its teaching into actual practice, they will be saved from the misery of being born in these evil realms of existence (*gatis*). The merit gained by one who practises it will be great indeed !"

He then ordered incense to be burnt, and all his disciples to pay homage to it and to recite it, so that they might realise the Essence of Mind. After they had recited it, all of them exclaimed, "Well done !"

At midnight, the Patriarch sent for Shen Hsiu to come to the hall, and asked him whether the stanza was written by him or not. "It was, Sir," replied Shen Hsiu. "I dare not be so vain as to expect to get the Patriarchate, but I wish Your Holiness would kindly tell me whether my stanza shows the least grain of wisdom."

"Your stanza," replied the Patriarch, "shows that you have not yet realised the Essence of Mind. So far you have reached the 'door of enlightenment,' but you have not yet entered it. To seek for supreme enlightenment with such an understanding as yours can hardly be successful.

"To attain supreme enlightenment, one must be able to know spontaneously one's own nature or Essence of Mind, which is neither created nor can it be annihilated. From ksana to ksana (thought-moment to thought-moment), one should be able to realise the Essence of Mind all the time. All things will then be free from restraint (i.e., emancipated). Once the Tathata (Suchness, another name for the Essence of Mind) is known, one will be free from delusion for ever ; and in all circumstances one's mind will be in a state of 'Thusness.' Such a state of mind is absolute Truth. If you can see things in such a frame of mind you will have known the Essence of Mind, which is supreme enlightenment.

"You had better go back to think it over again for a couple of days, and then submit me another stanza. If your stanza shows that you have entered the 'door of enlightenment,' I will transmit you the robe and the Dharma."

Shen Hsiu made obeisance to the Patriarch and left. For several days, he tried in vain to write another stanza. This upset his mind so much that he was as ill at ease as if he were in a nightmare, and he could find comfort neither in sitting nor in walking.

Two days after, it happened that a young boy who was passing by the room where I was pounding rice recited loudly the stanza written by Shen Hsiu. As soon as I heard it, I knew at once that the composer of it had not yet realised the Essence of Mind. For although I had not been taught about it at that time, I already had a general idea of it.

"What stanza is this?" I asked the boy. "You barbarian," he replied, "don't you know about it ? The Patriarch told his disciples that the question of incessant rebirth was a momentous one, that those who wished to inherit his robe and Dharma should write him a stanza, and that the one who had an understanding of the Essence of Mind would get them and be made the Sixth Patriarch. Elder Shen Hsiu wrote this 'Formless' Stanza on the wall of the south corridor and the Patriarch told us to recite it. He also said that those who put its teaching into actual practice would attain great merit, and be saved from the misery of being born in the evil realms of existence."

I told the boy that I wished to recite the stanza too, so that I might have an affinity with its teaching in future life. I also told him that although I had been pounding rice there for eight months I had never been to the hall, and that he would have to show me where the stanza was to enable me to make obeisance to it.

The boy took me there and I asked him to read it to me, as I am illiterate. A petty officer of the Chiang Chou District named Chang Tih-Yung, who happened to be there, read it out to me. When he had finished reading I told him that I also had composed a stanza, and asked him to write it for me. "Extraordinary indeed," he exclaimed, "that you also can compose a stanza !"

"Don't despise a beginner," said I, "if you are a seeker of supreme enlightenment. You should know that the lowest class may have the sharpest wit, while the highest may be in want of intelligence. If you slight others, you commit a very great sin."

"Dictate your stanza," said he. "I will take it down for you. But do not forget to deliver me, should you succeed in getting the Dharma !"

My stanza read :
> There is no Bodhi-tree,
> Nor stand of a mirror bright.
> Since all is void,
> Where can the dust alight ?

When he had written this, all disciples and others who were present were greatly surprised. Filled with admiration, they said to one another, "How wonderful ! No doubt we should not judge people by appearance. How can it be that for so long we have made a Bodhisattva incarnate work for us ?"

Seeing that the crowd was overwhelmed with amazement, the Patriarch rubbed off the stanza with his shoe, lest jealous ones should do me injury. He expressed the opinion, which they took for granted, that the author of this stanza had also not yet realised the Essence of Mind.

Next day the Patriarch came secretly to the room where the rice was pounded. Seeing that I was working there with a stone pestle, he said to me, "A seeker of the Path risks his life for the Dharma. Should he not do so ?" Then he asked, "Is the rice ready ?" "Ready long ago," I replied, "only waiting for the sieve." He knocked the mortar thrice with his stick and left.

Knowing what his message meant, in the third watch of the night I went to his room. Using the robe as a screen so that none could see us, he expounded the Diamond Sutra to me. When he came to the sentence, "One should use one's mind in such a way that it will be free from any attachment,"* I at once became thoroughly enlightened, and realised that all things in the universe are the Essence of Mind itself.

"Who would have thought," I said to the Patriarch, "that the Essence of Mind is intrinsically pure ! Who would

* Note by Dhyana Master Hui An :
" 'To be free from any attachment' means not to abide in form or matter, not to abide in sound, not to abide in delusion, not to abide in enlightenment, not to abide in the quintessence, not to abide in the attribute. 'To use the mind' means to let the 'One Mind' (i.e., the Universal mind) manifest itself everywhere. When we let our mind dwell on piety or on evil, piety

18

have thought that the Essence of Mind is intrinsically free from becoming or annihilation ! Who would have thought that the Essence of Mind is intrinsically self-sufficient ! Who would have thought that the Essence of Mind is intrinsically free from change ! Who would have thought that all things are the manifestation of the Essence of Mind!"

Knowing that I had realised the Essence of Mind, the Patriarch said, "For him who does not know his own mind there is no use learning Buddhism. On the other hand, if he knows his own mind and sees intuitively his own nature, he is a Hero, a 'Teacher of gods and men,' 'Buddha'."

Thus, to the knowledge of no one, the Dharma was transmitted to me at midnight, and consequently I became the inheritor of the teaching of the 'Sudden' School as well as of the robe and the begging bowl.

"You are now the Sixth Patriarch," said he. "Take good care of yourself, and deliver as many sentient beings as possible. Spread and preserve the teaching, and don't let it come to an end. Take note of my stanza :

Sentient beings who sow the seeds of enlightenment
In the field of causation will reap the fruit of Buddhahood.
Inanimate objects void of Buddha-nature
Sow not and reap not.

He further said, "When the Patriarch Bodhidharma first came to China, most Chinese had no confidence in him, and so this robe was handed down as a testimony from one Patriarch to another. As to the Dharma, this is transmitted from heart to heart, and the recipient must realise it by his

or evil manifests itself, but our Essence of Mind (or Primordial mind) is thereby obscured. But when our mind dwells on nothing, we realise that all the worlds of the ten quarters are nothing but the manifestation of 'One Mind.'

"The above commentary is most accurate and to the point. Scholastic Buddhist scholars can never give an explanation as satisfactory as this. For this reason Dhyana Masters (National Teacher Hui An being one of them) are superior to the so-called Scriptural Expounders."

DIH PING TSZE.

own efforts. From time immemorial it has been the practice for one Buddha to pass to his successor the quintessence of the Dharma, and for one Patriarch to transmit to another the esoteric teaching from heart to heart. As the robe may give cause for dispute, you are the last one to inherit it. Should you hand it down to your successor, your life would be in imminent danger. Now leave this place as quickly as you can, lest some one should do you harm."

"Whither should I go ?" I asked. "At Huai you stop and at Hui you seclude yourself," he replied.

Upon receiving the robe and the begging bowl in the middle of the night, I told the Patriarch that, being a Southerner, I did not know the mountain tracks, and that it was impossible for me to get to the mouth of the river (to catch a boat). "You need not worry," said he. "I will go with you."

He then accompanied me to Kiukiang, and there ordered me into a boat. As he did the rowing himself, I asked him to sit down and let me handle the oar. "It is only right for me to carry you across," he said (an allusion to the sea of birth and death which one has to go across before the shore of Nirvana can be reached). To this I replied, "While I am under illusion, it is for you to get me across ; but after enlightenment, I should cross it by myself. (Although the term 'to go across' is the same, it is used differently in each case). As I happen to be born on the frontier, even my speaking is incorrect in pronunciation, (but in spite of this) I have had the honour to inherit the Dharma from you. Since I am now enlightened, it is only right for me to cross the sea of birth and death myself by realising my own Essence of Mind."

"Quite so, quite so," he agreed. "Beginning from you the Dhyana School will become very popular. Three years after your departure from me I shall leave this world. You may start on your journey now. Go as fast as you can towards the South. Do not preach too soon, as Buddhism is not so easily spread."

20

After saying good-bye, I left him and walked towards the South. In about two months' time, I reached the Ta Yü Mountain. There I noticed that several hundred men were in pursuit of me with the intention of robbing me of my robe and begging bowl.

Among them there was a monk named Hui Ming, whose lay surname was Ch'en. He was a general of the fourth rank in lay life. His manner was rough and his temper hot. Of all the pursuers, he was the most vigilant in search of me. When he was about to overtake me, I threw the robe and the begging bowl on a rock, saying, "This robe is nothing but a symbol. What is the use of taking it away by force ?" (I then hid myself). When he got to the rock, he tried to pick them up, but found he could not. Then he shouted out, "Lay Brother, Lay Brother, (for the Patriarch had not yet formally joined the Order) I come for the Dharma, not for the robe."

Whereupon I came out from my hiding place and squatted on the rock. He made obeisance and said, "Lay Brother, preach to me, please."

"Since the object of your coming is the Dharma," said I, "refrain from thinking of anything and keep your mind blank. I will then teach you." When he had done this for a considerable time, I said, "When you are thinking of neither good nor evil, what is at that particular moment, Venerable Sir, your real nature (literally, original face) ?"

As soon as he heard this, he at once became enlightened. But he further asked, "Apart from those esoteric sayings and esoteric ideas handed down by the Patriarch from generation to generation, are there any other esoteric teachings ?" "What I can tell you is not esoteric," I replied. "If you turn your light inwardly,* you will find what is esoteric within you."

"In spite of my staying in Huang Mei," said he, "I did not realise my self-nature. Now thanks to your guidance, I know it as a water-drinker knows how hot or how cold the water is. Lay Brother, you are now my teacher."

I replied, "If that is so, then you and I are fellow disciples of the Fifth Patriarch. Take good care of yourself."

In answering his question whither he should go thereafter, I told him to stop at Yuan and to take up his abode in Meng. He paid homage and departed.

Sometime after I reached Ts'ao Ch'i. There the evildoers again persecuted me and I had to take refuge in Szu Hui, where I stayed with a party of hunters for a period as long as fifteen years.

Occasionally I preached to them in a way that befitted their understanding. They used to put me to watch their nets, but whenever I found living creatures therein I set them free. At meal times I put vegetables in the pan in which they cooked their meat. Some of them questioned me, and I explained to them that I would eat the vegetables only, after they had been cooked with the meat.

One day I bethought myself that I ought not to pass a secluded life all the time, and that it was high time for me to propagate the Law. Accordingly I left there and went to the Fa Hsin Temple in Canton.

At that time Bhikkhu Yin Tsung, Master of the Dharma, was lecturing on the Maha Parinirvana Sutra in the Temple. It happened that one day, when a pennant was blown about by the wind, two Bhikkhus entered into a dispute as to what it was that was in motion, the wind or the pennant. As they could not settle their difference I submitted to them that it was

* The most important point in the teaching of the Dhyana School lies in 'Introspection,' which means the turning of one's own 'light' to reflect inwardly. To illustrate, let us take the analogy of a lamp. We know that the light of a lamp, when surrounded by a shade, will reflect inwardly with its radiance centering on itself, whereas the rays of a naked flame will diffuse and shine outwardly. Now when we are engrossed with criticising others, as is our wont, we hardly turn our thoughts on ourselves, and hence scarcely know anything about ourselves. Contrary to this, the followers of the Dhyana School turn their attention completely within and reflect exclusively on their own 'real nature,' known in Chinese as one's 'original face.'

Lest our readers should overlook this important passage, let it be noted that in China alone thousands of Buddhists have attained enlightenment by acting on this wise saying of the Sixth Patriarch.

DIH PING TSZE.

neither, and that what actually moved was their own mind. The whole assembly was startled by what I said, and Bhikkhu Yin Tsung invited me to take a seat of honour and questioned me about various knotty points in the Sutras.

Seeing that my answers were precise and accurate, and that they showed something more than book-knowledge, he said to me, "Lay Brother, you must be an extraordinary man. I was told long ago that the inheritor of the Fifth Patriarch's robe and Dharma had come to the South. Very likely you are the man."

To this I politely assented. He immediately made obeisance and asked me to show the assembly the robe and the begging bowl which I had inherited.

He further asked what instructions I had when the Fifth Patriarch transmitted me the Dharma. "Apart from a discussion on the realisation of the Essence of Mind," I replied, "he gave me no other instruction, nor did he refer to Dhyana and Emancipation." "Why not ?" he asked. "Because that would mean two ways," I replied. "And there cannot be two ways in Buddhism. There is one way only."

He asked what was the only way. I replied, "The Maha Parinirvana Sutra which you expound explains that Buddha-nature is the only way. For example, in that Sutra King Kao Kuei-Teh, a Bodhisattva, asked Buddha whether or not those who commit the four acts of gross misconduct,† or the five deadly sins,* and those who are *icchantika* (heretics) etc., would eradicate their 'element of goodness' and their Buddha-nature. Buddha replied, 'There are two kinds of 'element of goodness,' the eternal and the non-eternal. Since Buddha-nature is neither eternal nor non-eternal, therefore their 'element of goodness' is not eradicated. Now Buddhism is known as having no two ways. There are good ways and evil ways, but since

† Killing, stealing, carnality and lying.
* Patricide, matricide, setting the Buddhist Order in discord, killing an Arhat, and causing blood to flow from the body of a Buddha.

Buddha-nature is neither, therefore Buddhism is known as having no two ways. From the point of view of ordinary folks, the component parts of a personality (*skandhas*) and factors of consciousness (*dhatus*) are two separate things : but enlightened men understand that they are not dual in nature. Buddha-nature is non-duality."

Bhikkhu Yin Tsung was highly pleased with my answer. Putting his two palms together as a sign of respect, he said, "My interpretation of the Sutra is as worthless as a heap of debris, while your discourse is as valuable as genuine gold." Subsequently he conducted the ceremony of hair-cutting for me (*i.e.*, the ceremony of Initiation into the Order) and asked me to accept him as my pupil.

Thenceforth, under the Bodhi-tree I preached the teaching of the Tung Shan School (the School of the Fourth and the Fifth Patriarchs, who lived in Tung Shan).

Since the time when the Dharma was transmitted to me in Tung Shan, I have gone through many hardships and my life often seemed to be hanging by a thread. Today, I have had the honour of meeting you in this assembly, and I must ascribe this to our good connection in previous *kalpas* (cyclic periods), as well as to our common accumulated merits in making offerings to various Buddhas in our past reincarnations ; otherwise, we should have had no chance of hearing the above teaching of the 'Sudden' School, and thereby laying the foundation of our future success in understanding the Dharma.

This teaching was handed down from the past Patriarchs, and it is not a system of my own invention. Those who wish to hear the teaching should first purify their own mind, and after hearing it they should each clear up their own doubts in the same way as the Sages did in the past."

At the end of the address, the assembly felt rejoiced, made obeisance and departed.

CHAPTER II

ON PRAJNA

NEXT day Prefect Wei asked the Patriarch to give another address. Thereupon, having taken his seat and asked the assembly to purify their mind collectively, and to recite the Maha Prajnaparamita Sutra, he gave the following address :

Learned Audience, the Wisdom of Enlightenment (Bodhiprajna) is inherent in every one of us. It is because of the delusion under which our mind works that we fail to realise it ourselves, and that we have to seek the advice and the guidance of enlightened ones before we can know our own Essence of Mind. You should know that so far as Buddhanature is concerned, there is no difference between an enlightened man and an ignorant one. What makes the difference is that one realises it, while the other is ignorant of it. Now, let me talk to you about Maha Prajnaparamita, so that each of you can attain wisdom.

Learned Audience, those who recite the word 'Prajna' the whole day long do not seem to know that Prajna is inherent in their own nature. But mere talking on food will not appease hunger, and this is exactly the case with these people. We might talk on Sunyata (the Void) for myriads of kalpas, but talking alone will not enable us to realise the Essence of Mind, and it serves no purpose in the end.

The word 'Mahaprajnaparamita' is Sanskrit, and means 'great wisdom to reach the opposite shore' (of the sea of existence). What we have to do is to put it into practice with our mind ; whether we recite it or not does not matter. Mere reciting it without mental practice may be likened to a phantasm, a magical delusion, a flash of lightning or a dewdrop. On the other hand, if we do both, then our mind will be in accord with what we repeat orally. Our very nature is Buddha, and apart from this nature there is no other Buddha.

What is Maha ? It means 'great.' The capacity of the mind is as great as that of space. It is infinite, neither round nor square, neither great nor small, neither green nor yellow, neither red nor white, neither above nor below, neither long nor short, neither angry nor happy, neither right nor wrong, neither good nor evil, neither first nor last. All Buddha ksetras (lands) are as void as space. Intrinsically our transcendental nature is void and not a single dharma (thing) can be attained. It is the same with the Essence of Mind, which is a state of 'Absolute Void' (*i.e.*, the voidness of non-void).

Learned Audience, when you hear me talk about the Void, do not at once fall into the idea of vacuity, (because this involves the heresy of the doctrine of annihilation). It is of the utmost importance that we should not fall into this idea, because when a man sits quietly and keeps his mind blank he will abide in a state of 'Voidness of Indifference.'

Learned Audience, the illimitable Void of the universe is capable of holding myriads of things of various shape and form, such as the sun, the moon, stars, mountains, rivers, worlds, springs, rivulets, bushes, woods, good men, bad men, dharmas pertaining to goodness or badness, deva planes, hells, great oceans, and all the mountains of the Mahameru. Space takes in all these, and so does the voidness of our nature. We say that the Essence of Mind is great because it embraces all things, since all things are within our nature. When we see the goodness or the badness of other people we are not attracted by it, nor repelled by it, nor attached to it ; so that our attitude of mind is as void as space. In this way, we say our mind is great. Therefore we call it 'Maha.'

Learned Audience, what the ignorant merely talk about, wise men put into actual practice with their mind. There is also a class of foolish people who sit quietly and try to keep their mind blank. They refrain from thinking of anything and call themselves 'great.' On account of their heretical view we can hardly talk to them.

Learned Audience, you should know that the mind is very

great in capacity, since it pervades the whole Dharmadhatu (the sphere of the Law, *i.e.*, the Universe). When we use it, we can know something of everything, and when we use it to its full capacity we shall know all. All in one and one in all. When our mind works without hindrance, and is at liberty to 'come' or to 'go,' then it is in a state of 'Prajna.'

Learned Audience, all Prajna comes from the Essence of Mind and not from an exterior source. Have no mistaken notion about that. This is called 'Self-use of the True Nature.' Once the Tathata (Suchness, the Essence of Mind) is known, one will be free from delusion forever.

Since the scope of the mind is for great objects, we should not practise such trivial acts (as sitting quietly with a blank mind). Do not talk about the 'Void' all day without practising it in the mind. One who does this may be likened to a self-styled king who is really a commoner. Prajna can never be attained in this way, and those who behave like this are not my disciples.

Learned Audience, what is Prajna ? It means 'Wisdom.' If at all times and in all places we steadily keep our thought free from foolish desire, and act wisely on all occasions, then we are practising Prajna. One foolish notion is enough to shut off Prajna, while one wise thought will bring it forth again. People in ignorance or under delusion do not see it; they talk about it with their tongues, but in their mind they remain ignorant. They are always saying that they practise Prajna, and they talk incessantly on 'Voidness'; but they do not know the 'Absolute Void.' 'The Heart of Wisdom' is Prajna, which has neither form nor characteristic. If we interpret it in this way, then indeed it is the wisdom of Prajna.

What is Paramita ? It is a Sanskrit word, meaning 'to the opposite shore.' Figuratively, it means 'above existence and non-existence.' By clinging to sense objects, existence or non-existence arises like the up and down of the billowy sea, and such a state is called metaphorically 'this shore' ; while by non-attachment a state above existence and non-existence, like smoothly running water, is attained, and this

27

is called 'the opposite shore.' This is why it is called 'Paramita.'

Learned Audience, people under illusion recite the 'Mahaprajnaparamita' with their tongues, and while they are reciting it erroneous and evil thoughts arise. But if they put it into practice unremittingly, they realise its 'true nature.' To know this Dharma is to know the Dharma of Prajna, and to practise this is to practise Prajna. He who does not practise it is an ordinary man. He who directs his mind to practise it even for one moment is the equal of Buddha.

For ordinary man *is* Buddha, and klesa (defilement) is Bodhi (enlightenment). A foolish passing thought makes one an ordinary man, while an enlightened second thought makes one a Buddha. A passing thought that clings to sense-objects is klesa, while a second thought that frees one from attachment is Bodhi.

Learned Audience, the Mahaprajnaparamita is the most exalted, the supreme, and the foremost. It neither stays, nor goes, nor comes. By means of it Buddhas of the present, the past, and the future generations attain Buddhahood. We should use this great wisdom to break up the five skandhas,* for to follow such a practice ensures the attainment of Buddhahood. The three poisonous elements (greed, hatred and illusion) will then be turned into Sila (good conduct), Samadhi and Prajna.

Learned Audience, in this system of mine one Prajna produces eighty-four thousand ways of wisdom, since there are that number of 'defilements' for us to cope with ; but when one is free from defilements, wisdom reveals itself, and will not be separated from the Essence of Mind. Those who understand this Dharma will be free from idle thoughts. To be free from being infatuated by one particular thought, from clinging to desire, and from falsehood ; to put one's

---

* Material qualities, or matter, sensation, perception, dispositions or tendencies, and consciousness.

own essence of Tathata into operation ; to use Prajna for contemplation, and to take an attitude of neither indifference nor attachment towards all things—this is what is meant by realising one's own Essence of Mind for the attainment of Buddhahood.

Learned Audience, if you wish to penetrate the deepest mystery of the Dharmadhatu and the Samadhi of Prajna, you should practise Prajna by reciting and studying the Vajracchedika (The Diamond) Sutra, which will enable you to realise the Essence of Mind.   You should know that the merit for studying this Sutra, as distinctly set forth in the text, is immeasurable and illimitable, and cannot be enumerated in details.   This Sutra belongs to the highest School of Buddhism, and the Lord Buddha delivered it specially for the very wise and quick-witted.   If the less wise and the slow-witted should hear about it they would doubt its credibility.   Why ?   For example, if it rained in Jambudvipa (the Southern Continent), through the miracle of the celestial Naga, cities, towns, and villages would drift about in the flood as if they were only leaves of the date tree.   But should it rain in the great ocean the level of the sea as a whole would not be affected by it.   When Mahayanists hear about the Diamond Sutra their minds become enlightened ;   they know that Prajna is immanent in their Essence of Mind and that they need not rely on scriptural authority, since they can make use of their own wisdom by constant practice of contemplation.

The Prajna immanent in the Essence of Mind of every one may be likened to the rain, the moisture of which refreshes every living thing, trees and plants as well as sentient beings.   When rivers and streams reach the sea, the water carried by them merges into one body ;   this is another analogy.   Learned Audience, when rain comes in a deluge, plants which are not deep-rooted are washed away, and eventually they succumb.   This is the case with the slow-witted, when they hear about the teaching of the 'Sudden' School.   The Prajna immanent in them is exactly the same as that in the very wise men, but they fail to enlighten themselves when the Dharma is made known to them. Why ? Because they are thickly veiled by erroneous views and deep-rooted defilements, in the same way as the sun may be thickly veiled by cloud and unable to show his light until the wind blows the cloud away.

Prajna does not vary with different persons ; what makes the difference is whether one's mind is enlightened or deluded. He who does not know his own Essence of Mind, and is under the delusion that Buddhahood can be attained by outward religious rites is called the slow-witted. He who knows the teaching of the 'Sudden' School and attaches no importance to rituals, and whose mind functions always under right views, so that he is absolutely free from defilements or contaminations, is said to have known his Essence of Mind.

Learned Audience, the mind should be framed in such a way that it will be independent of external or internal objects, at liberty to come or go, free from attachment and thoroughly enlightened without the least beclouding. He who is able to do this is of the same standard required by the Sutras of the Prajna School.

Learned Audience, all sutras and scriptures of the Mahayana and Hinayana Schools, as well as the twelve sections of the canonical writings, were provided to suit the different needs and temperaments of various people. It is upon the principle that Prajna is latent in every man that the doctrines expounded in these books are established.

If there were no human beings, there would be no Dharmas ; hence we know that all Dharmas are made for men, and that all Sutras owe their existence to the preachers. Since some men are wise, the so-called superior men, and some are ignorant, the so-called inferior men, the wise preach to the ignorant when the latter ask them to do so. Through this the ignorant may attain sudden enlightenment, and their mind thereby becomes illuminated. Then they are no longer different from the wise men.

Learned Audience, without enlightenment there would be no difference between a Buddha and other living beings ; while a gleam of enlightenment is enough to make any living being the equal of a Buddha. Since all Dharmas are immanent in our mind there is no reason why we should not realise intuitively the real nature of Tathata (Suchness). The Bodhisattva Sila Sutra says, "Our Essence of Mind is intrinsically pure, and if we knew our mind and realised what our nature is, all of us would attain Buddhahood." As the Vimalakirti Nirdesa Sutra says, "At once they become enlightened and regain their own mind."

Learned Audience, when the Fifth Patriarch preached to me I became enlightened immediately after he had spoken, and spontaneously realised the real nature of Tathata. For this reason it is my particular object to propagate the teaching of this 'Sudden' School, so that learners may find Bodhi at once and realise their true nature by introspection of mind.

Should they fail to enlighten themselves, they should ask the pious and learned Buddhists who understand the teaching of the Highest School to show them the right way. It is an exalted position, the office of a pious and learned Buddhist who guides others to realise the Essence of Mind. Through his assistance one may be initiated into all meritorious Dharmas. The wisdom of the past, the present and the future Buddhas as well as the teachings of the twelve sections of the Canon are immanent in our mind ; but in case we fail to enlighten ourselves, we have to seek the guidance of the pious and learned ones. On the other hand, those who enlighten themselves need no extraneous help. It is wrong to insist upon the idea that without the advice of the pious and learned we cannot obtain liberation. Why ? Because it is by our innate wisdom that we enlighten ourselves, and even the extraneous help and instructions of a pious and learned friend would be of no use if we were deluded by false doctrines and erroneous views. Should we introspect our mind with real Prajna, all erroneous views would be vanquished in a moment, and as soon as we know the Essence of Mind we arrive immediately at the Buddha stage.

Learned Audience, when we use Prajna for introspection we are illumined within and without, and in a position to know our own mind. To know our mind is to obtain liberation. To obtain liberation is to attain Samadhi of Prajna, which is 'thoughtlessness.' What is 'thoughtlessness'? 'Thoughtlessness' is to see and to know all Dharmas (things) with a mind free from attachment. When in use it pervades everywhere, and yet it sticks nowhere. What we have to do is to purify our mind so that the six vijnanas (aspects of consciousness), in passing through the six gates (sense organs) will neither be defiled by nor attached to the six sense-objects. When our mind works freely without any hindrance, and is at liberty to 'come' or to 'go,' we attain Samadhi of Prajna, or liberation. Such a state is called the function of 'thoughtlessness.' But to refrain from thinking of anything, so that all thoughts are suppressed, is to be Dharma-ridden, and this is an erroneous view.

Learned Audience, those who understand the way of 'thoughtlessness' will know everything, will have the experience all Buddhas have had, and attain Buddhahood. In future, if an initiate of my School should make a vow in company with his fellow-disciples to devote his whole life without retrogression to the practice of the teachings of this 'Sudden' School, in the same spirit as that for serving Buddha, he would reach without failure the Path of Holiness. (To the right men) he should transmit from heart to heart the instructions handed down from one Patriarch to another; and no attempt should be made to conceal the orthodox teaching. To those who belong to other schools, and whose views and objects are different from ours, the Dharma should not be transmitted, since it will be anything but good for them. This step is taken lest ignorant persons who cannot understand our system should make slanderous remarks about it and thereby annihilate their seed of Buddha-

32

nature for hundreds of kalpas and thousands of incarnations.

Learned Audience, I have a 'formless' stanza for you all to recite. Both laity and monks should put its teaching into practice, without which it would be useless to remember my words alone. Listen to this stanza :

A master of the Buddhist Canon as well as of the teaching of the Dhyana School
May be likened unto the blazing sun sitting high in his meridian tower.
Such a man would teach nothing but the Dharma for realising the Essence of Mind,
And his object in coming to this world would be to vanquish the heretical sects.
We can hardly classify the Dharmas into 'Sudden' and 'Gradual,'
But some men will attain enlightenment much quicker than others.
For example, this system for realising the Essence of Mind
Is above the comprehension of the ignorant.
We may explain it in ten thousand ways,
But all those explanations may be traced back to one principle.
To illumine our gloomy tabernacle, which is stained by defilement,
We should constantly set up the Light of Wisdom.
Erroneous views keep us in defilement
While right views remove us from it,
But when we are in a position to discard both of them
We are then absolutely pure.
Bodhi is immanent in our Essence of Mind,
An attempt to look for it elsewhere is erroneous.
Within our impure mind the pure one is to be found,
And once our mind is set right, we are free from the three kinds of beclouding (hatred, lust and illusion).
If we are treading the Path of Enlightenment
We need not be worried by stumbling-blocks.
Provided we keep a constant eye on our own faults
We cannot go astray from the right path.
Since every species of life has its own way of salvation
They will not interfere with or be antagonistic to one another.

But if we leave our own path and seek some other way of
    salvation
We shall not find it,
And though we plod on till death overtakes us
We shall find only penitence in the end.
If you wish to find the true way
Right action will lead you to it directly;
But if you do not strive for Buddhahood
You will grope in the dark and never find it.
He who treads the Path in earnest
Sees not the mistakes of the world;
If we find fault with others
We ourselves are also in the wrong.
When other people are in the wrong, we should ignore it,
For it is wrong for us to find fault.
By getting rid of the habit of fault-finding
We cut off a source of defilement.
When neither hatred nor love disturb our mind
Serenely we sleep.
Those who intend to be the teachers of others
Should themselves be skilled in the various expedients which
    lead others to enlightenment.
When the disciple is free from all doubts
It indicates that his Essence of Mind has been found.
The Kingdom of Buddha is in this world,
Within which enlightenment is to be sought.
To seek enlightenment by separating from this world
Is as absurd as to search for a rabbit's horn.
Right views are called 'transcendental' ;
Erroneous views are called 'worldly.'
When all views, right or erroneous, are discarded
Then the essence of Bodhi appears.
This stanza is for the 'Sudden' School.
It is also called the 'Great Ship of Dharma' (for sailing across
    the ocean of existence).
Kalpa after kalpa a man may be under delusion,
But once enlightened it takes him only a moment to attain
    Buddhahood.

Before conclusion, the Patriarch added, "Now, in this
Ta Fan Temple, I have addressed you on the teaching of

the 'Sudden' School. May all sentient beings of the Dharmadhatu instantly understand the Law and attain Buddhahood."

After hearing what the Patriarch said, the Prefect Wei, government officials, Taoists and laymen were all enlightened. They made obeisance in a body and exclaimed unanimously, "Well done ! Well done ! Who would have expected that a Buddha was born in Kwangtung ?"

CHAPTER III

QUESTIONS AND ANSWERS

ONE day Prefect Wei entertained the Patriarch and asked him to preach to a big gathering At the end of the feast, Prefect Wei asked him to mount the pulpit (to which the Patriarch consented). After bowing twice reverently, in company with other officials, scholars, and commoners, Prefect Wei said, "I have heard what Your Holiness preached. It is really so deep that it is beyond our mind and speech, and I have certain doubts which I hope you will clear up for me." "If you have any doubts," replied the Patriarch, "please ask, and I will explain."

"What you preach are the fundamental principles taught by Bodhidharma, are they not ?" "Yes," replied the Patriarch. "I was told," said Prefect Wei, "that at Bodhidharma's first interview with Emperor Wu of Liang he was asked what merits the Emperor would get for the work of his life in building temples, allowing new monks to be ordained (royal consent was necessary at that time), giving alms and entertaining the Order ; and his reply was that these would bring no merits at all. Now, I cannot understand why he gave such an answer. Will you please explain."

"These would bring no merits," replied the Patriarch. "Don't doubt the words of the Sage. Emperor Wu's mind was under an erroneous impression, and he did not know the orthodox teaching. Such deeds as building temples, allowing new monks to be ordained, giving alms and entertaining the Order will bring you only felicities, which should not be taken for merits. Merits are to be found within the Dharmakaya, and they have nothing to do with practices for attaining felicities."

The Patriarch went on, "Realisation of the Essence of Mind is Kung (good deserts), and equality is Têh (good quality). When our mental activity works without any impediment, so that we are in a position to know constantly the true state and the mysterious functioning of our own mind, we are said to have acquired Kung Têh (merits).

Within, to keep the mind in a humble mood is Kung ; and without, to behave oneself according to propriety is Têh. That all things are the manifestation of the Essence of Mind is Kung, and that the quintessence of mind is free from idle thoughts is Têh. Not to go astray from the Essence of Mind is Kung, and not to pollute the mind in using it is Têh. If you seek for merits within the Dharmakaya, and do what I have just said, what you acquire will be real merits. He who works for merits does not slight others ; and on all occasions he treats everybody with respect. He who is in the habit of looking down upon others has not got rid of the erroneous idea of a self, which indicates his lack of Kung. Because of his egotism and his habitual contempt for all others, he knows not the real Essence of Mind ; and this shows his lack of Têh. Learned Audience, when our mental activity works without interruption, then it is Kung ; and when our mind functions in a straightforward manner, then it is Têh. To train our own mind is Kung, and to train our own body is Têh. Learned Audience, merits should be sought within the Essence of Mind and they cannot be acquired by almsgiving, entertaining the monks etc. We should therefore distinguish between felicities and merits. There is nothing wrong in what our Patriarch said. It is Emperor Wu himself who did not know the true way."

Prefect Wei then asked the next question. "I notice that it is a common practice for monks and laymen to recite the name of Amitabha with the hope of being born in the Pure Land of the West. To clear up my doubts, will you please tell me whether it is possible for them to be born there or not."

"Listen to me carefully, Sir," replied the Patriarch, "and I will explain. According to the Sutra spoken by the Bhagavat in Shravasti City for leading people to the Pure Land of the West, it is quite clear that the Pure Land is not far from here, for the distance in mileage is 108,000, which really represents the 'ten evils' and 'eight errors' within us. To those of inferior mentality certainly it is far away, but to

37

superior men we may say that it is quite near. Although the Dharma is uniform, men vary in their mentality. Because they differ from one another in their degree of enlightenment or ignorance, therefore some understand the Law quicker than others. While ignorant men recite the name of Amitabha and pray to be born in the Pure Land, the enlightened purify their mind, for, as the Buddha said, 'When the mind is pure, the Buddha Land is simultaneously pure.'

"Although you are a native of the East, if your mind is pure you are sinless. On the other hand, even if you were a native of the West an impure mind could not free you from sin. When the people of the East commit a sin, they recite the name of Amitabha and pray to be born in the West ; but in the case of sinners who are natives of the West, where should they pray to be born ? Ordinary men and ignorant people understand neither the Essence of Mind nor the Pure Land within themselves, so they wish to be born in the East or the West. But to the enlightened everywhere is the same. As the Buddha said, 'No matter where they happen to be, they are always happy and comfortable.'

"Sir, if your mind is free from evil the West is not far from here; but difficult indeed it would be for one whose heart is impure to be born there by invoking Amitabha !

"Now, I advise you, Learned Audience, first to do away with the 'ten evils' ; then we shall have travelled one hundred thousand miles. For the next step, do away with the 'eight errors,' and this will mean another eight thousand miles traversed. If we can realise the Essence of Mind at all times and behave in a straightforward manner on all occasions, in the twinkling of an eye we may reach the Pure Land and there see Amitabha.

"If you only put into practice the ten good deeds, there would be no necessity for you to be born there. On the other hand, if you do not do away with the 'ten evils' in your mind, which Buddha will take you there ? If you understand the Birthless Doctrine (which puts an end to the cycle of birth and death) of the 'Sudden' School, it takes

you only a moment to see the West. If you do not understand, how can you reach there by reciting the name of
Amitabha, as the distance is so far ?

"Now, how would you like it if I were to shift the Pure
Land to your presence this very moment, so that all of you
might see it ?" The congregation made obeisance and
replied, "If we might see the Pure Land here there would be
no necessity for us to desire to be born there. Will Your
Holiness kindly let us see it by having it removed here."

The Patriarch said, "Sirs, this physical body of ours is a
city. Our eyes, ears, nose, and tongue are the gates. There
are five external gates, while the internal one is ideation.
The mind is the ground. The Essence of Mind is the King
who lives in the domain of the mind. While the Essence of
Mind is in, the King is in, and our body and mind exist.
When the Essence of Mind is out, there is no King and our
body and mind decay. We should work for Buddhahood
within the Essence of Mind, and we should not look for it
apart from ourselves. He who is kept in ignorance of his
Essence of Mind is an ordinary being. He who is enlightened in his Essence of Mind is a Buddha. To be
merciful is Avalokitesvara (one of the two principal Bodhisattvas of the Pure Land). To take pleasure in almsgiving
is Mahasthama (the other Bodhisattva). Competence for a
pure life is Sakyamuni (one of the titles of Gautama Buddha).
Equality and straightforwardness is Amitabha. The idea
of a self or that of a being is Mount Meru. A depraved
mind is the ocean. Klesa (defilement) is the billow. Wickedness is the evil dragon. Falsehood is the devil. The
wearisome sense objects are the aquatic animals. Greed
and hatred are the hells. Ignorance and infatuation are
the brutes.

"Learned Audience, if you constantly perform the ten
good deeds, paradise will appear to you at once. When
you get rid of the idea of a self and that of a being, Mount
Meru will topple. When the mind is no longer depraved,
the ocean (of existence) will be dried up. When you are

39

free from klesa, billows and waves (of the ocean of existence) will calm down. When wickedness is alien to you, fish and evil dragons will die out.

"Within the domain of our mind, there is a Tathagata of Enlightenment who sends forth a powerful light which illumines externally the six gates (of sensation) and purifies them. This light is strong enough to pierce through the six Kama Heavens (heavens of desire) ; and when it is turned inwardly it eliminates at once the three poisonous elements, purges away our sins which might lead us to the hells or other evil realms, and enlightens us thoroughly within and without, so that we are no different from those born in the Pure Land of the West. Now, if we do not train ourselves up to this standard, how can we reach the Pure Land ?"

Having heard what the Patriarch said, the congregation knew their Essence of Mind very clearly. They made obeisance and exclaimed in one voice, "Well done !" They also chanted, "May all the sentient beings of this Universe who have heard this sermon at once understand it intuitively."

The Patriarch added, "Learned Audience, those who wish to train themselves (spiritually) may do so at home. It is quite unnecessary for them to stay in monasteries. Those who train themselves at home may be likened unto a native of the East who is kind-hearted, while those who stay in monasteries but neglect their work differ not from a native of the West who is evil in heart. So far as the mind is pure, it is the 'Western Pure Land of one's own Essence of Mind.' "

Prefect Wei asked, "How should we train ourselves at home ? Will you please teach us."

The Patriarch replied, "I will give you a 'formless' stanza. If you put its teaching into practice you will be in the same position as those who live with me permanently. On the other hand, if you do not practise it, what progress can you make in the spiritual path, even though you cut your hair and leave home for good (*i.e.*, join the Order) ? The stanza reads :

For a fair mind, observation of precepts (Sila) is unnecessary.
For straightforward behaviour, practice in Dhyana (contempla-
tion) may be dispensed with.
On the principle of gratefulness, we support our parents
and serve them filially.
On the principle of righteousness, the superior and the inferior
stand for each other (in time of need).
On the principle of mutual desire to please, the senior and the
junior are on affectionate terms.
On the principle of forbearance, we do not quarrel even in
the midst of a hostile crowd.
If we can persevere till fire can be obtained through rubbing
a piece of wood,
Then the red lotus (the Buddha-nature) will shoot out from
the black mire (the unenlightened state).
That which is of bitter taste is bound to be good medicine.
That which sounds unpleasant to the ear is certainly frank
advice.
By amending our mistakes, we get wisdom.
By defending our faults, we betray an unsound mind.
In our daily life, we should always practise altruism,
But Buddhahood is not to be attained by giving away money
as charity.
Bodhi is to be found within our own mind,
And there is no necessity to look for mysticism from without.
Hearers of this stanza who put its teaching into actual practice
Will find paradise in their very presence.

The Patriarch added, "Learned Audience, all of you should
put into practice what is taught in this stanza, so that you
can realise the Essence of Mind and attain Buddhahood
directly. The Dharma waits for no one. I am going back
to Ts'ao Ch'i, so the assembly may now break up. If
you have any questions, you may come there to put them."

At this juncture Prefect Wei, the government officials,
pious men, and devout ladies who were present were all
enlightened. Faithfully they accepted the teaching and
put it into practice.

CHAPTER IV

SAMADHI AND PRAJNA

THE Patriarch on another occasion preached to the assembly as follows :

Learned Audience, in my system (Dhyana) Samadhi and Prajna are fundamental. But do not be under the wrong impression that these two are independent of each other, for they are inseparably united and are not two entities. Samadhi is the quintessence of Prajna, while Prajna is the activity of Samadhi. At the very moment that we attain Prajna, Samadhi is therewith ; and vice versa. If you understand this principle, you understand the equilibrium of Samadhi and Prajna. A disciple should not think that there is a distinction between 'Samadhi begets Prajna' and 'Prajna begets Samadhi.' To hold such an opinion would imply that there are two characteristics in the Dharma.

For one whose tongue is ready with good words but whose heart is impure, Samadhi and Prajna are useless, because they do not balance each other. On the other hand, when we are good in mind as well as in words, and when our outward appearance and our inner feelings harmonise with each other, then it is a case of equilibrium of Samadhi and Prajna.

Argument is unnecessary for an enlightened disciple. To argue whether Prajna or Samadhi comes first would put one in the same position as those who are under delusion. Argument implies a desire to win, strengthens egotism, and ties us to the belief in the idea of 'a self, a being, a living being, and a person.'

Learned Audience, to what are Samadhi and Prajna analogous ? They are analogous to a lamp and its light. With the lamp, there is light. Without it, it would be darkness. The lamp is the quintessence of the light and the light is the expression of the lamp. In name they are two things, but in substance they are one and the same. It is the same case with Samadhi and Prajna.

On another occasion the Patriarch preached to the assembly as follows :

Learned Audience, to practise the 'Samadhi of Specific Mode' is to make it a rule to be straightforward on all occasions—no matter whether we are walking, standing, sitting, or reclining. The Vimalakirti Nirdesa Sutra says, "Straightforwardness is the holy place, the Pure Land." Don't let your mind be crooked and practise straightforwardness with your lips only. We should practise straightforwardness and should not attach ourselves to anything. People under delusion believe obstinately in Dharmalaksana (things and form) and so they are stubborn in having their own way of interpreting the 'Samadhi of Specific Mode,' which they define as 'sitting quietly and continuously without letting any idea arise in the mind.' Such an interpretation would rank us with inanimate objects, and is a stumbling block to the right Path which must be kept open. Should we free our mind from attachment to all 'things,' the Path becomes clear ; otherwise, we put ourselves under restraint.* If that interpretation 'sitting quietly and continuously, etc.' be correct, why on one occasion was Sariputra reprimanded by Vimalakirti for sitting quietly in the wood ?†

* A Bhikkhu once asked Dhyana Master Shih T'ou, a successor to one of the Sixth Patriarch's disciples, "What is emancipation?" The Master asked him in return, "Who puts you under restraint ?" The significance of this answer is practically the same as that of our text here. Again, when the Sixth Patriarch said that the Fifth Patriarch would not discuss Dhyana and Emancipation but only the realisation of the Essence of Mind (Chapter I), he expressed the same idea. DIH PING TSZE.

† Vimalakirti said to Sariputra, "As to sitting quietly, it should mean that one does not put in an appearance within the three worlds (i.e., one's consciousness should be above the world of Desire, the world of Matter and the world of Non-Matter). It should mean that while remaining in Nirodha Samapatti (ecstacy with cessation of consciousness), one is able to do the various bodily movements such as walking, standing, sitting, or reclining etc. It should mean that without deviating from the Norm one is able to discharge various temporal duties. It should mean that one abides neither within nor without. It should mean that one practises the thirty-seven Bodhipaksa (Wings of Enlightenment) without being moved by heretical views. It should mean that without exterminating klesas (defilements) one may enter Nirvana. He who is able to sit thus will be approved by the Buddha."
VIMALAKIRTI NIRDESA SUTRA.

Learned Audience, some teachers of meditation instruct their disciples to keep a watch on their mind for tranquillity, so that it will cease from activity. Henceforth the disciples give up all exertion of mind. Ignorant persons become insane from having too much confidence in such instruction. Such cases are not rare, and it is a great mistake to teach others to do this.

(On another occasion) the Patriarch addressed the assembly as follows :

In orthodox Buddhism the distinction between the 'Sudden' School and the 'Gradual' School does not really exist ; the only difference is that by nature some men are quick-witted, while others are dull in understanding. Those who are enlightened realise the truth in a sudden, while those who are under delusion have to train themselves gradually. But such a difference will disappear when we know our own mind and realise our own nature. Therefore these terms, gradual and sudden, are more apparent than real.

Learned Audience, it has been the tradition of our school to take 'Idea-lessness' as our object, 'Non-objectivity' as our basis, and 'Non-attachment' as our fundamental principle. 'Idea-lessness' means not to be carried away by any particular idea in the exercise of the mental faculty. 'Non-objectivity' means not to be absorbed by objects when in contact with objects. 'Non-attachment' is the characteristic of our Essence of Mind.

All things—good or bad, beautiful or ugly—should be treated as void. Even in time of disputes and quarrels we should treat our intimates and our enemies alike and never think of retaliation. In the exercise of our thinking faculty, let the past be dead. If we allow our thoughts, past, present, and future, to link up in a series, we put ourselves under restraint. On the other hand, if we never let our mind attach to anything, we shall gain emancipation. For this reason, we take 'Non-attachment' as our fundamental principle.

To free ourselves from absorption in external objects is called 'Non-objectivity.' When we are in a position to do so, the nature of Dharma will be pure. For this reason, we take 'Non-objectivity' as our basis.

To keep our mind free from defilement under all circumstances is called "Idea-lessness.' Our mind should stand aloof from circumstances, and on no account should we allow them to influence the function of our mind. But it is a great mistake to suppress our mind from all thinking ; for even if we succeed in getting rid of all thoughts, and die immediately thereafter, still we shall be reincarnated elsewhere. Mark this, treaders of the Path. It is bad enough for a man to commit blunders from not knowing the meaning of the Law, but how much worse would it be to encourage others to follow suit ? Being deluded, he sees not and in addition he blasphemes the Buddhist Canon. Therefore we take 'Idea-lessness' as our object.

Learned Audience, let me explain more fully why we take 'Idea-lessness' as our object. It is because there is a type of man under delusion who boasts of the realisation of the Essence of Mind; but being carried away by circumstances, ideas rise in his mind, followed by erroneous views which are the source of all sorts of false notions and defilements. In the Essence of Mind (which is the embodiment of void), there is instrinsically nothing to be attained. To say that there is attainment, and to talk thoughtlessly on merits or demerits are erroneous views and defilements. For this reason we take 'Idea-lessness' as the object of our School.

Learned Audience, (in 'Idea-lessness') what should we get rid of and what should we fix our mind on ? We should get rid of the 'pairs of opposites' and all defiling conceptions. We should fix our mind on the true nature of Tathata (Suchness), for Tathata is the quintessence of idea, and idea is the result of the activity of Tathata.

It is the positive essence of Tathata—not the sense organs

45

—which give rise to 'idea.' Tathata bears its own attribute, and therefore it can give rise to 'idea.' Without Tathata the sense organs and the sense objects would perish immediately. Learned Audience, because it is the attribute of Tathata which gives rise to 'idea,' our sense organs—in spite of their functioning in seeing, hearing, touching, knowing etc.—need not be tainted or defiled in all circumstances, and our true nature may be 'self-manifested' all the time. Therefore the Sutra says, "He who is an adept in the discrimination of various Dharmalakshana (things and phenomena) will be immovably installed in the 'First Principle' (i.e., the blissful abiding place of the Holy, or Nirvana)."

CHAPTER V

DHYANA

The Patriarch (one day) preached to the assembly as follows:
In our system of meditation, we neither dwell upon the mind (in contradistinction to the Essence of Mind) nor upon purity. Nor do we approve of non-activity. As to dwelling upon the mind, the mind is primarily delusive; and when we realise that it is only a phantasm there is no need to dwell on it. As to dwelling upon purity, our nature is intrinsically pure ; and so far as we get rid of all delusive 'idea' there will be nothing but purity in our nature, for it is the delusive idea that obscures Tathata (Suchness). If we direct our mind to dwell upon purity we are only creating another delusion, the delusion of purity. Since delusion has no abiding place, it is delusive to dwell upon it. Purity has neither shape nor form ; but some people go so far as to invent the 'Form of Purity,' and treat it as a problem for solution. Holding such an opinion, these people are purity-ridden, and their Essence of Mind is thereby obscured.

Learned Audience, those who train themselves for 'imperturbability' should, in their contact with all types of men, ignore the faults of others. They should be indifferent to others' merit or demerit, good or evil, for such an attitude accords with the 'imperturbability of the Essence of Mind.' Learned Audience, a man unenlightened may be unperturbed physically, but as soon as he opens his mouth he criticises others and talks about their merits or demerits, ability or weakness, good or evil ; thus he deviates from the right course. On the other hand, to dwell upon our own mind or upon purity is also a stumbling-block in the Path.

The Patriarch on another occasion ·preached to the assembly as follows :
Learned Audience, what is sitting for meditation ? In our School, to sit means to gain absolute freedom and to be mentally unperturbed in all outward circumstances, be they

47

good or otherwise. To meditate means to realise inwardly the imperturbability of the Essence of Mind.

Learned Audience, what are Dhyana and Samadhi? Dhyana means to be free from attachment to all outer objects, and Samadhi means to attain inner peace. If we are attached to outer objects, our inner mind will be perturbed. When we are free from attachment to all outer objects, the mind will be in peace. Our Essence of Mind is intrinsically pure, and the reason why we are perturbed is because we allow ourselves to be carried away by the circumstances we are in. He who is able to keep his mind unperturbed, irrespective of circumstances, has attained Samadhi.

To be free from attachment to all outer objects is Dhyana, and to attain inner peace is Samadhi. When we are in a position to deal with Dhyana and to keep our inner mind in Samadhi, then we are said to have attained Dhyana and Samadhi. The Bodhisattva Sila Sutra says, "Our Essence of Mind is intrinsically pure." Learned Audience, let us realise this for ourselves at all times. Let us train ourselves, practise it by ourselves, and attain Buddhahood by our own effort.

CHAPTER VI

ON REPENTANCE

ONCE there was a big gathering of scholars and commoners from Kuang Chou, Shao Chou, and other places to wait upon the Patriarch to preach to them. Seeing this, the Patriarch mounted the pulpit and delivered the following address :

In Buddhism, we should start from our Essence of Mind. At all times let us purify our own mind from one thought-moment to another, treat the Path by our own efforts, realise our own Dharmakaya, realise the Buddha in our own mind, and deliver ourselves by a personal observance of Sila ; then your visit will not have been in vain. Since all of you have come from afar, the fact of our meeting here shows that there is a good affinity between us. Now let us sit down in the Indian fashion, and I will give you the five kinds of Incense of the Dharmakaya.

When they had sat down, the Patriarch continued: The first is the Sila Incense, which means that our mind is free from taints of misdeeds, evil, jealousy, avarice, anger, spoliation, and hatred. The second is the Samadhi Incense, which means that our mind is unperturbed in all circumstances, favourable or unfavourable. The third is the Prajna Incense, which means that our mind is free from all impediments, that we constantly introspect our Essence of Mind with wisdom, that we refrain from doing all kinds of evil deeds, that although we do all kinds of good acts, yet we do not let our mind become attached to (the fruits) of such actions, and that we are respectful towards our superiors, considerate to our inferiors, and sympathetic to the destitute and the poor. The fourth is the Incense of Liberation, which means that our mind is in such an absolutely free state that it clings to nothing and concerns itself neither with good nor evil. The fifth is the Incense of Knowledge obtained on the Attainment of Liberation. When our mind clings to neither good nor evil we should take care not to let it dwell upon vacuity, or remain in a state of inertia. Rather

49

should we enlarge our study and broaden our knowledge, so that we can know our own mind, understand thoroughly the principles of Buddhism, be congenial to others in our dealings with them, get rid of the idea of 'self' and that of 'being,' and realise that up to the time when we attain Bodhi the 'true nature' (or Essence of Mind) is always immutable. Such, then, is the Incense of Knowledge obtained on the Attainment of Liberation. This five-fold Incense fumigates us from within, and we should not look for it from without.

Now I will give you the 'formless' Repentance which will expiate our sins committed in our present, past, and future lives, and purify our karmas of thought, word and deed.

Learned Audience, please follow me and repeat together what I say.

May we, disciples so and so, be always free from the taints of ignorance and delusion. We repent of all our sins and evil deeds committed under delusion or in ignorance. May they be expiated at once and may they never arise again.

May we be always free from the taints of arrogance and dishonesty (Asatya). We repent of all our arrogant behaviour and dishonest dealings in the past. May they be expiated at once and may they never arise again.

May we be always free from the taints of envy and jealousy. We repent of all our sins and evil deeds committed in an envious or jealous spirit. May they be expiated at once and may they never arise again.

Learned Audience, this is what we call 'formless Ch'an Hui' (repentance). Now what is the meaning of Ch'an ? Ch'an refers to the repentance of past sins. To repent of all our past sins and evil deeds committed under delusion, ignorance, arrogance, dishonesty, jealousy, or envy, etc. so as to put an end to all of them is called Ch'an. Hui refers to that part of repentance concerning our future conduct. Having realised the nature of our transgression (we make a vow) that hereafter we will put an end to all kinds of evil committed under delusion, ignorance, arrogance, dishonesty, jealousy, or envy, and that we shall never sin again. This is Hui.

On account of ignorance and delusion, common people do not realise that in repentance they have not only to feel sorry for their past sins but also to refrain from sinning in the future. Since they take no heed of their future conduct they commit new sins before the past are expiated. How can we call this 'repentance' ?

Learned Audience, having repented of our sins we will take the following four All-embracing Vows.

We vow to deliver an infinite number of sentient beings of our mind.*

We vow to get rid of the innumerable defilements in our own mind.

We vow to learn the countless systems in Dharma of our Essence of Mind.

We vow to attain the Supreme Buddhahood of our Essence of Mind.

Learned Audience, all of us have now declared that we vow to deliver an infinite number of sentient beings ; but what does that mean ? It does not mean that I, Hui Neng, am going to deliver them. And who are these sentient beings within our mind ? They are the delusive mind, the deceitful mind, the evil mind, and such like minds— all these are sentient beings. Each of them has to deliver himself by means of his own Essence of Mind. Then the deliverance is genuine.

Now, what does it mean to deliver oneself by one's own Essence of Mind ? It means the deliverance of the ignorant, the delusive, and the vexatious beings within our mind by means of Right Views. With the aid of Right Views and Prajna-Wisdom the barriers raised by these ignorant and delusive beings may be broken down ; so that each of them is in a position to deliver himself by his own efforts. Let the fallacious be delivered by rightness ; the deluded by enlightenment ; the ignorant by wisdom ; and the malevol-

* Buddhists believe that all 'things' are nothing but phenomena in mind.

51

ent by benevolence. Such is genuine deliverance.

As to the vow, 'We vow to get rid of the innumerable evil passions in the mind,' it refers to the substitution of our unreliable and illusive thinking faculty by the Prajna-Wisdom of our Essence of Mind.

As to the vow, 'We vow to learn countless systems of Dharmas,' there will be no true learning until we have seen face to face our Essence of Mind, and until we conform to the orthodox Dharma on all occasions.

As to the vow, 'We vow to attain Supreme Buddhahood,' when we are able to bend our mind to follow the true and orthodox Dharma on all occasions, and when Prajna always rises in our mind, so that we can hold aloof from enlightenment as well as from ignorance, and do away with truth as well as falsehood, then we may consider ourselves as having realised the Buddha-nature, or in other words, as having attained Buddhahood.

Learned Audience, we should always bear in mind that we are treading the Path, for thereby strength will be added to our vows. Now, since all of us have taken these four All-embracing Vows, let me teach you the 'Formless Three-fold Guidance.'

We take 'Enlightenment' as our guide, because it is the culmination of both Punya (merit) and Prajna (wisdom).

We take 'Orthodoxy' (Dharma) as our guide, because it is the best way to get rid of desire.

We take 'Purity' as our guide, because it is the noblest quality of mankind.

Hereafter, let the Enlightened One be our teacher ; on no account should we accept Mara (the personification of evil) or any heretic as our guide. This we should testify to ourselves by constantly appealing to the 'Three Gems' of our Essence of Mind, in which, Learned Audience, I advise you to take refuge. They are :

Buddha, which stands for Enlightenment.

Dharma, which stands for Orthodoxy.

Sangha, (the Order) which stands for Purity.

To let our mind take refuge in 'Enlightenment,' so that evil and delusive notions do not arise, desire decreases, discontent is unknown, and lust and greed no longer bind, this is the culmination of Punya and Prajna.

To let our mind take refuge in 'Orthodoxy' so that we are always free from wrong views (for without wrong views there would be no egotism, arrogance, or craving), this is the best way to get rid of desire.

To let our mind take refuge in 'Purity' so that no matter in what circumstances it may be it will not be contaminated by wearisome sense-objects, craving and desire, this is the noblest quality of mankind.

To practise the Threefold Guidance in the way above mentioned means to take refuge in oneself (*i.e.*, in one's own Essence of Mind). Ignorant persons take the Three-fold Guidance day and night, but do not understand it. If they say they take refuge in Buddha, do they know where he is ? Yet if they cannot see Buddha, how can they take refuge in him ? Does not such an assertion amount to a lie ?

Learned Audience, each of you should consider and examine this point for yourself, and let not your energy be misapplied. The Sutra distinctly says that we should take refuge in the Buddha within ourselves ; it does not suggest that we should take refuge in other Buddhas. (Moreover), if we do not take refuge in the Buddha within ourselves, there is no other place for us to retreat.

Having cleared up this point, let each of us take refuge in the 'Three Gems' within our mind. Within, we should control our mind ; without, we should be respectful towards others—this is the way to take refuge within ourselves.

Learned Audience, since all of you have taken the 'Three-fold Guidance' I am going to speak to you on the Trikaya (three 'bodies') of the Buddha of our Essence of Mind, so that you can see these three bodies and realise clearly the Essence of Mind. Please listen carefully and repeat this after me :

With our physical body, we take refuge in the Pure Dharmakaya (Essence-body) of Buddha.

With our physical body, we take refuge in the Perfect Sambhogakaya (Manifestation body) of Buddha.

With our physical body, we take refuge in the Myriad Nirmanakaya (Incarnation-bodies) of Buddha.

Learned Audience, our physical body may be likened unto an inn (*i.e.*, a temporary abode), so we cannot take refuge there. Within our Essence of Mind these Trikaya of Buddha are to be found, and they are common to everybody. Because the mind (of an ordinary man) labours under delusions, he knows not his own inner nature ; and the result is that he ignores the Trikaya within himself, (erroneously believing) that they are to be sought from without. Please listen, and I will show you that within yourself you will find the Trikaya which, being the manifestation of the Essence of Mind, are not to be sought from without.

Now, what is the Pure Dharmakaya ? Our Essence of Mind is intrinsically pure ; all things are only its manifestations, and good deeds and evil deeds are only the result of good thoughts and evil thoughts respectively. Thus, within the Essence of Mind all things (are intrinsically pure), like the azure of the sky and the radiance of the sun and the moon which, when obscured by passing clouds, may appear as if their brightness had been dimmed ; but as soon as the clouds are blown away, brightness re-appears and all objects are fully illuminated. Learned Audience, our evil habits may be likened unto the clouds ; while sagacity and wisdom (Prajna), are the sun and the moon respectively. When we attach ourselves to outer objects, our Essence of Mind is clouded by wanton thoughts which prevent our Sagacity and Wisdom from sending forth their light. But should we be fortunate enough to find learned and pious teachers to make known to us the Orthodox Dharma, then we may with our own efforts do away with ignorance and delusion, so that we are enlightened both within and without, and the (true nature) of all things manifests itself within our

Essence of Mind. This is what happens to those who have seen face to face the Essence of Mind, and this is what is called the Pure Dharmakaya of Buddha.

Learned Audience, to take refuge in a true Buddha is to take refuge in our own Essence of Mind. He who does so should remove from his Essence of Mind the evil mind, the jealous mind, the flattering and crooked mind, egotism, deceit and falsehood, contemptuousness, snobbishness, fallacious views, arrogance, and all other evils that may arise at any time. To take refuge in ourself is to be constantly on the alert for our own mistakes, and to refrain from criticism of others' merits or faults. He who is humble and meek on all occasions and is polite to everybody has thoroughly realised his Essence of Mind, so thoroughly that his Path is free from further obstacles. This is the way to take refuge in ourself.

What is the Perfect Sambhogakaya ? Let us take the illustration of a lamp. Even as the light of a lamp can break up darkness which has been there for a thousand years, so a spark of Wisdom can do away with ignorance which has lasted for ages. We need not bother about the past, for the past is gone and irrecoverable. What demands our attention is the future ; so let our thoughts from moment to moment be clear and round, and let us see face to face our Essence of Mind. Good and evil are opposite to each other, but their quintessence cannot be dualistic. This non-dualistic nature is called the true nature which can neither be contaminated by evil nor affected by good. This is what is called the Sambhogakaya of Buddha.

One single evil thought from our Essence of Mind will spoil the good merits accumulated in aeons of time, while a good thought from that same source can expiate all our sins, though they are as many as the grains of sand in the Ganges. To realise our own Essence of Mind from moment to moment without intermission until we attain Supreme Enlightenment, so that we are perpetually in a state of Right Mindfulness, is the Sambhogakaya.

Now, what is the Myriad Nirmanakaya ? When we subject ourselves to the least discrimination or particularization, transformation takes place ; otherwise, all things remain as void as space, as they inherently are. By dwelling our mind on evil things, hell arises. By dwelling our mind on good acts, paradise appears. Dragons and snakes are the transformation of venomous hatred, while Bodhisattvas are mercy personified. The upper regions are Prajna crystallized, while the underworld is only another form assumed by ignorance and infatuation. Numerous indeed are the transformations of the Essence of Mind ! People under delusion awake not and understand not ; always they bend their minds on evil, and as a rule practise evil. But should they turn their minds from evil to righteousness, even for a moment, Prajna would instantly arise. This is what is called the Nirmanakaya of the Buddha of the Essence of Mind.

Learned Audience, the Dharmakaya is intrinsically self-sufficient. To see face to face from moment to moment our own Essence of Mind is the Sambhogakaya of Buddha. To dwell our mind on the Sambhogakaya (so that Wisdom or Prajna arises) is the Nirmanakaya. To attain enlightenment by our own efforts and to practise by ourself the goodness inherent in our Essence of Mind is a genuine case of 'Taking Refuge.' Our physical body, consisting of flesh and skin, etc., is nothing more than a tenement, (for temporary use only), so we do not take refuge therein. But let us realise the Trikaya of our Essence of Mind, and we shall know the Buddha of our Essence of Mind.

I have a 'formless' stanza, the reciting and practising of which will at once dispel the delusions and expiate the sins accumulated in numerous kalpas. This is the stanza :

People under delusion accumulate tainted merits but do not tread the Path.
They are under the impression that to accumulate merits and to tread the Path are one and the same thing.

Though their merits for alms-giving and offerings are infinite
(They do not realize that) the ultimate source of sin lies in
the three poisonous elements (i.e., greed, anger and illusion)
within their own mind.
They expect to expiate their sins by accumulating merit
Without knowing that felicities obtained in future lives have
nothing to do with the expiation of sins.
Why not get rid of the sin within our own mind,
For this is true repentance (within our Essence of Mind) ?
(A sinner) who realises suddenly what constitutes true repent-
ance according to the Mahayana School,
And who ceases from doing evil and practises righteousness
is free from sin.
A treader of the Path who keeps a constant watch on his
Essence of Mind
May be classified in the same group as the various Buddhas.
Our Patriarchs transmitted no other system of Law but this
'Sudden' one.
May all followers of it see face to face their Essence of Mind
and be at once with the Buddhas.
If you are going to look for the Dharmakaya
See it above Dharmalaksana (phenomena), and then your Mind
will be pure.
Exert yourself in order to see face to face the Essence of Mind,
and relax not,
For death may come suddenly and put an abrupt end to
your earthly existence.
Those who understand the Mahayana teaching and are thus
able to realise the Essence of Mind
Should reverently put their palms together (as a sign of respect)
and fervently seek for the Dharmakaya.

The Patriarch then added :
Learned Audience, all of you should recite this stanza
and put it into practice. Should you realise your Essence
of Mind after reciting it, you may consider yourself to be
always in my presence, though actually you are a thousand
miles away, but should you be unable to do so, then, though
we are face to face, we are really a thousand miles apart.
In that case, what is the use of taking the trouble to come here

57

from so far away ? Take good care of yourselves. Good-bye.

The whole assembly, after hearing what the Patriarch had said, became enlightened. In a very happy mood, they accepted his teaching and put it into practice.

CHAPTER VII

TEMPERAMENT AND CIRCUMSTANCES

Instructions given according to the disciples' temperament and to the circumstances of the case

Upon the Patriarch's return to the village of Ts'ao Hou in Shao Chou from Huang Mei, where the Dharma had been transmitted to him, he was still an unknown figure, and it was a Confucian scholar named Liu Chih-Lüeh who gave him a warm welcome. Chih-Lüeh happened to have an aunt named Wu Chin-Tsang who was a bhikkhuni (a female member of the Order), and used to recite the Maha-Parinirvana Sutra. After hearing the recitation for only a short while the Patriarch grasped its profound meaning and began to explain it to her. Whereupon, she picked up the book and asked him the meaning of certain words.

"I am illiterate," he replied, "but if you wish to know the purport of this work, please ask." "How can you grasp the meaning of the text," she rejoined, "when you do not even know the words?" To this he replied, "The profundity of the teachings of the various Buddhas has nothing to do with the written language."

This answer surprised her very much, and realising that he was no ordinary bhikkhu, she made it widely known to the pious elders of the village. "This is a holy man," she said, "we should ask him to stay, and get his permission to supply him food and lodging."

Whereupon, a descendant of Marquis Wu of the Wei Dynasty, named Ts'ao Shu-Liang, came one afternoon with other villagers to tender homage to the Patriarch. The historical Pao Lin monastery, devastated by war at the end of the Sui Dynasty, was then reduced to a heap of ruins, but on the old site they rebuilt it and asked the Patriarch to stay there. Before long, it became a very famous monastery.

After being there for nine months his wicked enemies traced him and persecuted him again. Thereupon he took refuge in a nearby hill. The villains then set fire to the wood (where he was hiding), but he escaped by making his way to a rock. This rock, which has since been known as the 'Rock of Refuge,' has thereon the knee-prints of the Patriarch and also the impressions of the texture of his gown.

Recollecting the instruction of his master, the Fifth Patriarch, that he should stop at Huai and seclude himself at Hui, he made these two districts his places of retreat.

Bhikkhu Fa Hai, a native of Chü Kiang of Shao Chow, in his first interview with the Patriarch asked the meaning of the well-known saying, 'What mind is, Buddha is.' The Patriarch replied, "To let not a passing thought rise up is 'mind.' To let not the coming thought be annihilated is Buddha. To manifest all kinds of phenomena is 'mind.' To be free from all forms (*i.e.*, to realise the unreality of phenomena) is Buddha. If I were to give you a full explanation, the topic could not be exhausted even if I took up the whole of one kalpa. So listen to my stanza :

Prajna is 'What mind is,'
Samadhi is 'What Buddha is.'
In practising Prajna and Samadhi, let each keep pace with the other ;
Then our thoughts will be pure.
This teaching can be understood
Only through the habit of practice.
Samadhi functions, but inherently it does not become.
The orthodox teaching is to practise Prajna as well as Samadhi

After hearing what the Patriarch had said, Fa Hai was at once enlightened. He praised the Patriarch with the following stanza :

'What mind is, Buddha is' is true indeed !
But I humiliate myself by not understanding it.
Now I know the principal cause of Prajna and Samadhi,
Both of which I shall practise to set me free from all forms.

Bhikkhu Fa Ta, a native of Hung Chou, who joined the Order at the early age of seven, used to recite the Saddharma Pundarika (Lotus of the Good Law) Sutra. When he came to pay homage to the Patriarch, he failed to lower his head to the ground. For his abbreviated courtesy the Patriarch reproved him, saying, "If you object to lower your head to the ground, would it not be better to do away with salutation entirely ? There must be something in your mind that makes you so puffed up. Tell me what you do in your daily exercise."

"Recite the Saddharma Pundarika Sutra," replied Fa Ta. "I have read the whole text three thousand times."

"Had you grasped the meaning of the Sutra," remarked the Patriarch, "you would not have assumed such a lofty bearing, even if you had read it ten thousand times. Had you grasped it, you would be treading the same Path as mine. What you have accomplished has already made you conceited, and moreover, you do not seem to realise that this is wrong. Listen to my stanza :

Since the object of ceremony is to curb arrogance
Why did you fail to lower your head to the ground ?
'To believe in a self' is the source of sin,
But 'to treat all attainment as void' attains merit incomparable!

The Patriarch then asked for his name, and upon being told that his name was Fa Ta (meaning Understanding the Law), he remarked, "Your name is Fa Ta, but you have not yet understood the Law." He concluded by uttering another stanza :

Your name is Fa Ta.
Diligently and steadily you recite the Sutra.
Lip-repetition of the text goes by the pronunciation only,
But he whose mind is enlightened by grasping the meaning
    is a Bodhisattva indeed !
On account of conditions which may be traced to our past lives
I will explain this to you.
If you only believe that Buddha speaks no words,
Then the Lotus will blossom in your mouth.

Having heard this stanza, Fa Ta became remorseful and apologised to the Patriarch. He added, "Hereafter, I will be humble and polite on all occasions. As I do not quite understand the meaning of the Sutra I recite, I am doubtful as to its proper interpretation. With your profound knowledge and high wisdom, will you kindly give me a short explanation ?"

The Patriarch replied, "Fa Ta, the Law is quite clear ; it is only your mind that is not clear. The Sutra is free from doubtful passages ; it is only your mind that makes them doubtful. In reciting the Sutra, do you know its principal object ?"

"How can I know, Sir," replied Fa Ta, "since I am so dull and stupid ? All I know is how to recite it word by word."

The Patriarch then said, "Will you please recite the Sutra, as I cannot read it myself. I will then explain its meaning to you."

Fa Ta recited the Sutra, but when he came to the chapter entitled 'Parables' the Patriarch stopped him, saying, "The key-note of this Sutra is to set forth the aim and object of a Buddha's incarnation in this world. Though parables and illustrations are numerous in this book, none of them goes beyond this pivotal point. Now, what is that object ? What is that aim ? The Sutra says, 'It is for a sole object, a sole aim, verily a lofty object and a lofty aim that the Buddha appears in this world.' Now that sole object, that sole aim, that lofty object, that lofty aim referred to is the 'sight' of Buddha-Knowledge.

"Common people attach themselves to objects without; and within, they fall into the wrong idea of 'vacuity.' When they are able to free themselves from attachment to objects when in contact with objects, and to free themselves from the fallacious view of annihilation on the doctrine of 'Void' they will be free from delusions within and from illusions without. He who understands this and whose mind is thus enlightened in an instant is said to have opened his eyes for the sight of Buddha-Knowledge.

"The word 'Buddha' is equivalent to 'Enlightenment,' which may be dealt with (as in the Sutra) under four heads :

To open the eyes for the sight of Enlightenment-knowledge.

To show the sight of Enlightenment-knowledge.

To awake to the sight of Enlightenment-knowledge.

To be firmly established in the Enlightenment-knowledge.

"Should we be able, upon being taught, to grasp and understand thoroughly the teaching of Enlightenment-knowledge, then our inherent quality or true nature, *i.e.*, the Enlightenment-knowledge, would have an opportunity to manifest itself. You should not misinterpret the text, and come to the conclusion that Buddha-knowledge is something special to Buddha and not common to us all because you happen to find in the Sutra this passage, 'To open the eyes for the sight of Buddha-knowledge, to show the sight of Buddha-knowledge, etc.' Such a misinterpretation would amount to slandering Buddha and blaspheming the Sutra. Since he is a Buddha, he is already in possession of this Enlightenment-knowledge and there is no occasion for himself to open his eyes for it. You should therefore accept the interpretation that Buddha-knowledge is the Buddha-knowledge of your own mind and not that of any other Buddha.

"Being infatuated by sense-object, and thereby shutting themselves from their own light, all sentient beings, tormented by outer circumstances and inner vexations, act voluntarily as slaves to their own desires. Seeing this, our Lord Buddha had to rise from his Samadhi in order to exhort them with earnest preaching of various kinds to suppress their desires and to refrain from seeking happiness from without, so that they might become the equals of Buddha. For this reason the Sutra says, 'To open the eyes for the sight of Buddha-knowledge, etc.'

"I advise people constantly to open their eyes for the Buddha-knowledge within their mind. But in their perversity they commit sins under delusion and ignorance ; they are kind in words, but wicked in mind ; they are greedy, malignant, jealous, crooked, flattering, egotistic, offensive to men and destructive to inanimate objects. Thus, they open their eyes for the 'Common-people-knowledge.' Should they rectify their heart, so that wisdom arises perpetually, the mind would be under introspection, and evil doing be replaced by the practice of good ; then they would initiate themselves into the Buddha-knowledge.

"You should therefore from moment to moment open your eyes, not for 'Common-people-knowledge' but for Buddha-knowledge, which is super-mundane, while the former is worldly. On the other hand, if you stick to the concept that mere recitation (of the Sutra) as a daily exercise is good enough, then you are infatuated like the yak by its own tail." (Yaks are known to have a very high opinion of their own tails.)

Fa Ta then said, "If that is so, we have only to know the meaning of the Sutra and there would be no necessity for us to recite it. Is that right, Sir ?"

"There is nothing wrong in the Sutra," replied the Patriarch, "so that you should refrain from reciting it. Whether sutra-reciting will enlighten you or not, or benefit you or not, all depends on yourself. He who recites the Sutra with the tongue and puts its teaching into actual practice with his mind 'turns round' the Sutra. He who recites it without putting it into practice is 'turned round' by the Sutra. Listen to my stanza :

"When our mind is under delusion, the Saddharma Pundarika Sutra 'turns us round.'
With an enlightened mind we 'turn round' the Sutra instead.
To recite the Sutra for a considerable time without knowing its principal object
Indicates that you are a stranger to its meaning.
The correct way to recite the Sutra is without holding any arbitrary belief ;

Otherwise, it is wrong.
He who is above 'affirmative' and 'negative'
Rides permanently in the White Bullock Cart (the Vehicle
of Buddha)."

Having heard this stanza, Fa Ta was enlightened and moved to tears. "It is quite true," he exclaimed, "that heretofore I was unable to 'turn round' the Sutra. It was rather the Sutra that 'turned' me round."

He then raised another point. "The Sutra says, 'From Sravakas (disciples) up to Bodhisattvas, even if they were to speculate with combined efforts they would be unable to comprehend the Buddha-knowledge.' But you, Sir, give me to understand that if an ordinary man realises his own mind, he is said to have attained the Buddha-knowledge. I am afraid, Sir, that with the exception of those gifted with superior mental dispositions, others may doubt your remark. Furthermore, three kinds of Carts are mentioned in the Sutra, namely, Carts yoked with goats (i.e., the vehicle of Sravakas), Carts yoked with deers (the vehicle of Pratyeka Buddhas), and Carts yoked with bullocks (the vehicle of Bodhisattvas). How are these to be distinguished from the White Bullock Carts ?"

The Patriarch replied, "The Sutra is quite plain on this point ; it is you who misunderstand it. The reason why Sravakas, Pratyeka Buddhas and Bodhisattvas cannot comprehend the Buddha-knowledge is because they speculate on it. They may combine their efforts to speculate, but the more they speculate, the farther they are from the truth. It was to ordinary men, not to other Buddhas, that Buddha Gautama preached this Sutra. As for those who cannot accept the doctrine he expounded, he let them leave the assembly. You do not seem to know that since we are already riding in the White Bullock Cart (the vehicle of Buddhas), there is no necessity for us to go out to look for the other three vehicles. Moreover, the Sutra tells you plainly that there is only the Buddha Vehicle, and that

65

there are no other vehicles, such as the second or the third. It is for the sake of this sole vehicle that Buddha had to preach to us with innumerable skilful devices, using various reasons and arguments, parables and illustrations, etc. Why can you not understand that the other three vehicles are makeshifts, for the past only ; while the sole vehicle, the Buddha Vehicle, is the ultimate, meant for the present ?

"The Sutra teaches you to dispense with the makeshifts and to resort to the ultimate. Having resorted to the ultimate, you will find that even the name 'ultimate' disappears. You should appreciate that you are the sole owner of these valuables and that they are entirely subject to your disposal.* When you are free from the arbitrary conception that they are the father's, or the son's, or that they are at so and so's disposal, you may be said to have learnt the right way to recite the Sutra. In that case from kalpa to kalpa the Sutra will be in your hand, and from morning to night you will be reciting the Sutra all the time."

Being thus awakened, Fa Ta praised the Patriarch, in a transport of great joy, with the following stanza :

The delusion that I have attained great merits by reciting the Sutra three thousand times over
Is all dispelled by an utterance of the Master of Ts'ao Ch'i (i.e., the Patriarch).
He who has not understood the object of a Buddha's incarnation in this world
Is unable to suppress the wild passions accumulated in many lives.
The three vehicles yoked by goat, deer and bullock respectively, are makeshifts only,
While the three stages, preliminary, intermediate, and final, in which the orthodox Dharma is expounded, are well set out, indeed.
How few appreciate that within the burning house itself (i.e., mundane existence)
The King of Dharma is to be found !

* An allusion to the chapter in the Sutra, entitled 'Parables,' exemplifying that Buddha-knowledge is innate in every man.

The Patriarch then told him that henceforth he might call himself a 'Sutra-reciting Bhikkhu.' After that interview, Fa Ta was able to grasp the profound meaning of Buddhism, yet he continued to recite the Sutra as before.

Bhikkhu Chih Tung, a native of Shao Chou of An Feng had read the Lankavatara Sutra a thousand times, but he could not understand the meaning of Trikaya and the four Prajnas. Thereupon, he called on the Patriarch for an interpretation.

"As to the Three Bodies," explained the Patriarch, "the pure Dharmakaya is your (essential) nature ; the perfect Sambhogakaya is your wisdom ; and the myriad Nirmana-kayas are your actions. If you deal with these Three Bodies apart from the Essence of Mind, there would be 'bodies without wisdom.' If you realise that these Three Bodies have no positive essence of their own (because they are only the properties of the Essence of Mind) you attain the Bodhi of the four Prajnas. Listen to my stanza :

"The Three Bodies are inherent in our Essence of Mind,
By development of which the four Prajnas are manifested.
Thus, without shutting your eyes and your ears to keep away
    from the external world
You may reach Buddhahood directly.
Now that I have made this plain to you
Believe it firmly, and you will be free from delusions for ever.
Follow not those who seek Enlightenment from without ;
These people talk about Bodhi all the time (but they never
    find it)."

"May I know something about the four Prajnas ?" asked Chih Tung. "If you understand the Three Bodies," replied the Patriarch, "you should understand the four Prajnas as well ; so your question is unnecessary. If you deal with the four Prajnas apart from the Three Bodies, there will be Prajnas without bodies, in which case they would not be Prajnas."

The Patriarch then uttered another stanza :

The Mirror-like Wisdom is pure by nature.
The Equality Wisdom frees the mind from all impediments.
The All-discerning Wisdom sees things intuitively without
going through the process of reasoning.
The All-Performing Wisdom has the same characteristics as
the Mirror-like Wisdom.

The first five vijnanas (consciousness dependent respectively upon the five sense organs) and the Alayavijnana
(Storage or Universal consciousness) are 'transmuted' to
Prajna in the Buddha stage ; while the klista-mano-vijnana
(soiled-mind consciousness or self-consciousness) and the
mano-vijnana (thinking consciousness), are transmuted in
the Bodhisattva stage.*

These so-called 'transmutations of vijnana' are only
changes of appelations and not a change of substance.†

When you are able to free yourself entirely from attachment to sense-objects at the time these so-called 'transmutations' take place, you will forever abide in the repeatedly-
arising Naga (dragon) Samadhi.

(Upon hearing this), Chih Tung realised suddenly the
Prajna of his Essence of Mind and submitted the following
stanza to the Patriarch :

Intrinsically, the three Bodies are within our Essence of Mind.
When our mind is enlightened the four Prajnas will appear
therein.
When Bodies and Prajnas absolutely identify with each other
We shall be able to respond (in accordance with their temperaments and dispositions) to the appeals of all beings, no
matter what forms they may assume.

* It is in the first, 'Mudita' or Joyous Stage, when a Bodhisattva realises the
voidness of self and dharma (things), that he 'transmutes' the klista-mano-
vijnana to the All-discerning Wisdom.   When Buddhahood is attained, the
first five vijnanas will be 'transmuted' to the All-performing Wisdom,
and the Alaya-vijnana to the Mirror-like Wisdom.

† In the Essence of Mind there is no such thing as 'transmutation.'   When
a man is enlightened, the term 'Prajna' is used ;   otherwise, the term 'vijnana'
is applied.   In other words, the word 'transmutation' is used in the figurative
sense only.

> To start by seeking for the Trikaya and the four Prajnas is to take an entirely wrong course (for being inherent in us they are to be realised and not to be sought).
> To try to 'grasp' or 'confine' them is to go against their intrinsic nature.
> Through you, Sir, I am now able to grasp the profundity of their meaning,
> And henceforth I may discard for ever their false and arbitrary names. (*Note* : Having grasped the spirit of a doctrine, one may dispense with the names used therein, since all names are makeshifts only).

Bhikkhu Chih Ch'ang, a native of Kuei Ch'i of Hsin Chou, joined the Order in his childhood, and was very zealous in his efforts to realise the Essence of Mind. One day, he came to pay homage to the Patriarch, and was asked by the latter whence and why he came.

"I have recently been to the White Cliff Mountain in Hung Chou," replied he, "to interview the Master Ta T'ung, who was good enough to teach me how to realise the Essence of Mind and thereby attain Buddhahood. But as I still have some doubts, I have travelled far to pay you respect. Will you kindly clear them up for me, Sir."

"What instruction did he give you ?" asked the Patriarch.

"After staying there for three months without being given any instruction, and being zealous for the Dharma, I went alone to his chamber one night and asked him what was my Essence of Mind. 'Do you see the illimitable void ?' he asked. 'Yes, I do,' I replied. Then he asked me whether the void had any particular form, and when I said that the void is formless and therefore cannot have any particular form, he said, 'Your Essence of Mind is like the void. To realise that nothing can be seen is right seeing. To realise that nothing is knowable is true knowledge. To realise that it is neither green nor yellow, neither long nor short, that it is pure by nature, that its quintessence is perfect and clear, is to realise the Essence of Mind and thereby attain Buddhahood, which is also called the Buddha-knowledge.'

As I do not quite understand his teaching, will you please enlighten me, Sir."

"His teaching indicates," said the Patriarch, "that he still retains the arbitrary concepts of views and knowledge, and this explains why he fails to make it clear to you. Listen to my stanza :

"To realise that nothing can be seen but to retain the concept of 'invisibility'

Is like the surface of the sun obscured by passing clouds.

To realise that nothing is knowable but to retain the concept of 'unknowability'

May be likened to a clear sky disfigured by a lightning flash.

To let these arbitrary concepts rise spontaneously in your mind

Indicates that you have misidentified the Essence of Mind, and that you have not yet found the skilful means to realise it.

If you realise for one moment that these arbitrary concepts are wrong,

Your own spiritual light will shine forth permanently."

Having heard this Chih Ch'ang at once felt that his mind was enlightened. Thereupon, he submitted the following stanza to the Patriarch :

To allow the concepts of invisibility and unknowability to rise in the mind

Is to seek Bodhi without freeing oneself from the concepts of phenomena.

He who is puffed up by the slightest impression, 'I am now enlightened,'

Is no better than he was when under delusion.

Had I not put myself at the feet of the Patriarch

I should have been bewildered without knowing the right way to go.

One day, Chih Ch'ang asked the Patriarch, "Buddha preached the doctrine of 'Three Vehicles' and also that of a 'Supreme Vehicle.' As I do not understand this, will you please explain ?"

The Patriarch replied, "(In trying to understand these), you should introspect your own mind and act independently of things and phenomena. The distinction of these four vehicles does not exist in the Dharma itself but in the differentiation of people's minds. To see, to hear, and to recite the sutra is the small vehicle. To know the Dharma and to understand its meaning is the middle vehicle. To put the Dharma into actual practice is the great vehicle. To und∵rstand thoroughly all Dharmas, to have absorbed them completely, to be free from all attachments, to be above phenomena, and to be in possession of nothing, is the Supreme Vehicle.

"Since the word 'yana' (vehicle) implies 'motion' (*i.e.*, putting into practice), argument on this point is quite unnecessary. All depends on self-practice, so you need not ask me any more. (But I may remind you that) at all times the Essence of Mind is in a state of 'Thusness.' "

Chih Ch'ang made obeisance and thanked the Patriarch. Henceforth, he acted as his attendant until the death of the Master.

Bhikkhu Chih Tao, a native of Nan Hai of Kwang Tung, came to the Patriarch for instruction, saying, "Since I joined the Order I have read the Maha Parinirvana Sutra for more than ten years, but I have not yet grasped its main idea. Will you please teach me?"

"Which part of it do you not understand?" asked the Patriarch.

"It is about this part, Sir, that I am doubtful : 'All things are impermanent, and so they belong to the Dharma of becoming and cessation (*i.e.*, Samskrita Dharma). When both becoming and cessation cease to operate, the bliss of perfect rest and cessation of changes (*i.e.*, Nirvana) arises.' "

"What makes you doubt?" asked the Patriarch.

"All beings have two bodies—the physical body and the Dharmakaya," replied Chih Tao. "The former is impermanent ; it exists and dies. The latter is permanent ; it knows not and feels not. Now the Sutra says, 'When both becoming and cessation cease to operate, the bliss of

71

perfect rest and cessation of changes arises.' I do not know which body ceases to exist and which body enjoys the bliss. It cannot be the physical body that enjoys, because when it dies the four material elements (*i.e.*, earth, water, fire and air) will disintegrate, and disintegration is pure suffering, the very opposite of bliss. If it is the Dharmakaya that ceases to exist, it would be in the same state as 'inanimate' objects, such as grass, trees, stones etc.; who will then be the enjoyer ?

"Moreover, Dharma-nature is the quintessence of 'becoming and cessation,' which manifests as the five skandhas (rupa, vedana, samjna, samskara, and vijnana). That is to say, with one quintessence there are five functions. The process of 'becoming and cessation' is everlasting. When function or operation arises from the quintessence, it becomes ; when the operation or function is absorbed back into the quintessence, it ceases to exist. If reincarnation is admitted, there would be no 'cessation of changes,' as in the case of sentient beings. If reincarnation is out of the question, then things will remain forever in a state of lifeless quintessence, like inanimate objects. If this is so, then under the limitations and restrictions of Nirvana even existence will be impossible to all beings ; what enjoyment could there be ?"

"You are a son of Buddha, (a bhikkhu)," said the Patriarch, "so why do you adopt the fallacious views of Eternalism and Annihilationism held by the heretics, and criticise the teaching of the Supreme Vehicle ?

"Your argument implies that apart from the physical body there is a Law body (Dharmakaya) ; and that 'perfect rest' and 'cessation of changes' may be sought apart from 'becoming and cessation.' Further, from the statement, 'Nirvana is everlasting joy,' you infer that there must be somebody to play the part of the enjoyer.

"Now it is exactly these fallacious views that make people crave for sensate existence and indulge in worldly pleasure. It is for these people, the victims of ignorance, who identify the union of five skandhas as the 'self,' and regard all other things as 'not-self' (literally, outer sense objects); who crave for individual existence and have an aversion to death ; who drift about in the whirlpool of life and death without realising the hollowness of mundane existence, which is only a dream or an illusion ; who commit themselves to unnecessary suffering by binding themselves to the wheel of re-birth ; who mistake the state of everlasting joy of Nirvana for a mode of suffering, and who are always after sensual pleasure ; it is for these people that the compassionate Buddha preached the real bliss of Nirvana.

"At any one moment, Nirvana has neither the phenomenon of becoming, nor that of cessation, nor even the ceasing of operation of becoming and cessation. It is the manifestation of 'perfect rest and cessation of changes,' but at the time of manifestation there is not even a concept of manifestation; so it is called the 'everlasting joy' which has neither enjoyer nor non-enjoyer.

"There is no such thing as 'one quintessence and five functions' (as you allege), and you are slandering Buddha and blaspheming the Law when you state that under such limitation and restriction of Nirvana existence is impossible to all beings. Listen to my stanza :

The Supreme Maha Parinirvana
Is perfect, permanent, calm, and illuminating.
Ignorant people miscall it death,
While heretics hold that it is annihilation.
Those who belong to the Sravaka Vehicle or the Pratyeka
    Buddha Vehicle
Regard it as 'Non-action.'
All these are mere intellectual speculations,
And form the basis of the sixty two fallacious views.
Since they are mere fictitious names invented for the occasion
They have nothing to do with the Absolute Truth.
Only those of super-eminent mind
Can understand thoroughly what Nirvana is, and take up the

attitude of neither attachment nor indifference towards it.*
They know that five skandhas

And the so-called 'ego' arising from the union of these skandhas,
Together with all external objects and forms
And the various phenomena of sound and voice
Are equally unreal, like a dream or an illusion.
They make no discrimination between a sage and an ordinary
man.
Nor do they have any arbitrary concept on Nirvana.
They are above 'affirmation' and 'negation' and they break
the barrier of the past, the present, and the future.
They use their sense organs, when occasion requires,
But the concept of 'using' does not arise.
They may particularize on all sorts of things,
But the concept of 'particularization' does not arise.
Even during the cataclysmic fire at the end of a kalpa, when
ocean-beds are burnt dry,
Or during the blowing of the catastrophic wind when one
mountain topples on another,
The real and everlasting bliss of 'perfect rest' and 'cessation
of changes'
Of Nirvana remains in the same state and changes not.
Here I am trying to describe to you something which is ineffable
So that you may get rid of your fallacious views.
But if you do not interpret my words literally
You may perhaps learn a wee bit of the meaning of Nirvana !

Having heard this stanza, Chih Tao was highly enlightened. In a rapturous mood he made obeisance and departed.

---

* While ordinary people are bewildered by the whirlpool of birth and death,
the Sravakas' and Pratyeka Buddhas' attitude towards it is one of detestation.
Neither of them is in the right. A treader of the Path does not cling to
sensate existence nor does he shun it deliberately. Because the idea of a
'self' and that of a 'person' are foreign to him, and because he takes up the
attitude of neither attachment nor aversion towards all things, freedom is
within his reach all the time and he is at ease in all circumstances. He may
go through the process of birth and death, but such a process can never
bind him, so to him the question of 'birth and death' is no question at all.
Such a man may be called a man of super-eminent mind. DIH PING TSZE.

Bhikkhu Hsing Ssü, a Dhyana Master, was born at An Chêng of Chi Chou of a Liu family. Upon hearing that the preaching of the Patriarch had enlightened a great number of people, he at once came to Ts'ao Ch'i to tender him homage, and ask him this question :

"What should a learner direct his mind to, so that his attainment cannot be rated by the (usual) 'stages of progress' ?"

"What work have you been doing ?" asked the Patriarch.

"Even the Noble Truths taught by various Buddhas I have not anything to do with," replied Hsing Ssü.

"What stage of progress are you in ?" asked the Patriarch.

"What stage of progress can there be, when I refuse to have anything to do with even the Noble Truths?" he retorted.

His repartee commanded the great respect of the Patriarch who made him the leader of the assembly.

One day the Patriarch told him that he should propagate the Law in his own district, so that the teaching might not come to an end. Thereupon, he returned to Ch'ing Yuan Mountain in his native district. The Dharma having been transmitted to him, he spread it widely and thus perpetuated the teaching of his Master. Upon his death, the post-humous title 'Dhyana Master Hung Chi' was conferred on him.

Bhikkhu Huai Jang, a Dhyana Master, was born of a Tu family in Chin Chou. Upon his first visit to 'National Teacher' Hui An of Sung-Shan Mountain, he was directed by the latter to go to Ts'ao Ch'i to interview the Patriarch.

Upon his arrival, and after the usual salutation, he was asked by the Patriarch whence he came.

"From Sung Shan," replied he.

"What thing is it (that comes) ? How did it come ?" asked the Patriarch.

"To say that it is similar to a certain thing is wrong," he retorted.

"Is it attainable by training ?" asked the Patriarch.

"It is not impossible to attain it by training ; but it is quite impossible to pollute it," he replied.

Thereupon, the Patriarch exclaimed, "It is exactly this unpolluted thing that all Buddhas take good care of. It is so for you, and it is so for me as well. Patriarch Prajnatara of India foretold that under your feet a colt* would rush forth and trample on the people of the whole world. I need not interpret this oracle too soon, as the answer should be found within your mind."

Being thereby enlightened, Huai Jang realised intuitively what the Patriarch had said. Henceforth, he became his attendant for a period of fifteen years ; and day by day his knowledge of Buddhism got deeper and deeper. Afterwards, he made his home in Nan Yüeh where he spread widely the teaching of the Patriarch. Upon his death, the posthumous title, "Dhyana Master Ta Hui (Great Wisdom) was conferred on him by imperial edict.

Dhyana Master Hsüan Chiao of Yung Chia was born of a Tai family in Wenchow. As a youth, he studied sutras and shastras and was well-versed in the teaching of samatha (inhibition or quietude) and vipasyana (contemplation or discernment) of the T'ien T'ai School. Through the reading of the Vimalakirti Nirdesa Sutra he realised intuitively the mystery of his own mind.

A disciple of the Patriarch by the name of Hsüan Ts'ê happened to pay him a visit. During the course of a long discussion, Hsüan Ts'ê noticed that the utterance of his friend agreed virtually with the sayings of the various Patriarchs. Thereupon he asked, "May I know the name of your teacher who transmitted the Dharma to you ?"

"I had teachers to instruct me," replied Hsüan Chiao, "when I studied the sutras and the shastras of the vaipulya section. But afterwards it was through the reading of the

* This refers to Huai Jang's famous disciple, Ma (Horse) Tsu, through whom the teaching of the Dhyana School was spread all over China.

Vimalakirti Nirdesa Sutra that I realised the significance of the Buddhacitta (the Buddha Mind) ; and I have not yet had any teacher to verify and confirm my knowledge."

"Before the time of Bhisma Garjitasvara Raja Buddha," Hsüan Ts'ê remarked, "it was possible (to dispense with the service of a teacher) ; but since that time, he who attains enlightenment without the aid and the confirmation of a teacher is a natural heretic."

"Will you, Sir, kindly act as my testifier," asked Hsüan Chiao.

"My words carry no weight," replied his friend, "but in Ts'ao Ch'i there is the Sixth Patriarch, to whom visitors in great numbers come from all directions with the common object of having the Dharma transmitted to them. Should you wish to go there, I shall be pleased to accompany you."

In due course they arrived at Ts'ao Ch'i and interviewed the Patriarch. Having circumambulated the Patriarch thrice, Hsüan Chiao stood still (*i.e.*, without making obeisance to the Master) with the Buddhist staff in his hand.

The Patriarch remarked : "As a Buddhist monk is the embodiment of three thousand moral precepts and eighty thousand minor disciplinary rules, I wonder where you come from and what makes you so conceited."

"The question of incessant re-births is a momentous one," replied he, "and as death may come at any moment (I have no time to waste on ceremony)."

"Why do you not realise the principle of 'birthlessness,' and thus solve the problem of the transiency of life ?" the Patriarch retorted.

Thereupon Hsüan Chiao remarked, "To realise the Essence of Mind is to be free from re-births ; and once this problem is solved, the question of transiency no longer exists."

"That is so, that is so," the Patriarch agreed.

At this stage, Hsüan Chiao gave in and made obeisance in full ceremony. After a short while he bid the Patriarch adieu.

"You are going away too quickly, aren't you ?" asked the Patriarch.

"How can there be 'quickness' when motion intrinsically exists not ?" he retorted.

"Who knows that motion exists not ?" asked the Patriarch.

"I hope you, Sir, will not particularize," he observed.

The Patriarch commended him for his thorough grasp of the notion of 'birthlessness'; but Hsüan Chiao remarked, "Is there a 'notion' in 'birthlessness ?"

"Without a notion, who can particularize ?" asked the Patriarch in turn.

"That which particularizes is not a notion," replied Hsüan Chiao.

"Well said !" exclaimed the Patriarch. He then asked Hsüan Chiao to delay his departure and spend a night there. Henceforth Hsüan Chiao was known to his contemporaries as the 'enlightened one who had spent a night with the Patriarch.'

Afterwards, he wrote the famous work, 'A Song on Spiritual Attainment,' which circulates widely. His post-humous title is 'Grand Master Wu Hsiang' (He who is above form or phenomena), and he was also called by his contemporaries 'Dhyana Master Chên Chiao' (He who is really enlightened).

Bhikkhu Chih Huang, a follower of the Dhyana School, after his consultation with the Fifth Patriarch (as to the progress of his work) considered himself as having attained samadhi. For twenty years he confined himself in a small temple and kept up the position all the time.

Hsüan Ts'ê, a disciple of the Sixth Patriarch on a meditation journey to the northern bank of Huang Ho, heard about him and called at his temple.

"What are you doing here ?" asked Hsüan Ts'ê.

"I am abiding in samadhi," replied his friend, Chih Huang.

"Abiding in samadhi, did you say ?" observed Hsüan Ts'ê "I wish to know whether you are doing it consciously or unconsciously. For if you are doing it unconsciously, it would mean that it is possible for all inanimate objects such as earthenware, stones, trees, and weeds, to attain samadhi. On the other hand, if you are doing it consciously, then all animate objects or sentient beings would be in samadhi also."

"When I am in samadhi," observed Chih Huang, "I know neither consciousness nor unconsciousness."

"If that is the case," said Hsüan Ts'ê, "it is perpetual samadhi ; in which state there is neither abiding nor leaving. That state which you can abide in or leave off is not the great Samadhi."

Chih Huang was dumbfounded. After a long while, he asked, "May I know who is your teacher ?"

"My teacher is the Sixth Patriarch of Ts'ao Ch'i," replied Hsüan Ts'ê.

"How does he define dhyana and samadhi ?" Chih Huang asked.

"According to his teaching," replied Hsüan Ts'ê, "the Dharmakaya is perfect and serene ; its quintessence and its function are in a state of Thusness. The five skandhas are intrinsically void and the six sense-objects are non-existent. There is neither abiding nor leaving in samadhi. There is neither quietude nor perturbation. The nature of dhyana is non-abiding, so we should get above the state of 'abiding in the calmness of dhyana.' The nature of dhyana is uncreative, so we should get above the notion of 'creating a state of dhyana.' The state of the mind may be likened unto space, but (it is infinite) and so it is without the limitation of the latter."

Having heard this, Chih Huang went immediately to Ts'ao Ch'i to interview the Patriarch. Upon being asked whence he came, he told the Patriarch in detail the conversation he had had with Hsüan Ts'ê.

"What Hsüan Ts'ê said is quite right," said the Patriarch.

"Let your mind be in a state such as that of the illimitable void, but do not attach it to the idea of 'vacuity.' Let it function freely. Whether you are in activity or at rest, let your mind abide nowhere. Forget the discrimination between a sage and an ordinary man. Ignore the distinction of subject and object. Let the Essence of Mind and all phenomenal objects be in a state of Thusness. Then you will be in samadhi all the time."

Chih Huang was thereby fully enlightened. What he had considered for the past twenty years as an attainment now vanished. On that night inhabitants of Ho Pei (the northern bank of the Yellow River) heard a voice in the air to the effect that Dhyana Master Chih Huang had on that day gained enlightenment.

Some time after Chih Huang bid the Patriarch adieu and returned to Ho Pei, where he taught a great number of men and women, monks as well as the laity.

A Bhikkhu once asked the Patriarch what sort of man could obtain the keynote of the teaching of Huang Mei. "He who understands the Buddha Dharma can get it," replied the Patriarch. "Have you, Sir, got it then?" asked the Bhikkhu. "I do not understand the Buddha Dharma," was his reply.

One day the Patriarch wanted to wash the robe which he had inherited, but could find no good stream for the purpose. Thereupon he walked to a place about five miles from the rear of the monastery, where he noticed that plants and trees grew profusely and the environment gave an air of good omen. He shook his staff (which makes a tinkling noise, as rings are attached to the top of it) and stuck it in the ground. Immediately water spurted out and before long a pool was formed.

While he was kneeling down on a rock to wash the robe, a bhikkhu suddenly appeared before him and tendered him homage.

"My name is Fang Pien," said he, "and I am a native of Szechuan. When I was in South India I met Patriarch Bodhiharma, who instructed me to return to China. 'The Womb of the Orthodox Dharma,' said he, 'together with the robe which I inherited from Mahakasyapa have now been transmitted to the Sixth Patriarch, who is now in Ts'ao Ch'i of Shao Chou. Go there to have a look at them and to pay your respect to the Patriarch.' After a long voyage, I have arrived. May I see the robe and the begging bowl you inherited ?"

Having shown him the two relics, the Patriarch asked him what line of work he was taking up. "I am pretty good at sculptural work," replied he. "Let me see some of your work then," demanded the Patriarch.

Fang Pien was confounded at the time, but after a few days he was able to complete a life-like statue of the Patriarch, about seven inches high, a master-piece of sculpture.

(Upon seeing the statue), the Patriarch laughed and said to Fang Pien, "You know something about the nature of sculptural work, but you do not seem to know the nature of Buddha." He then put his hand on Fang Pien's head (the Buddhist way of blessing) and declared, "You shall for ever be a 'field of merit' for human and celestial beings."

In addition, the Patriarch rewarded his service with a robe, which Fang Pien divided into three parts, one for dressing the statue, one for himself, and one for burying in the ground after covering it up with palm leaves. (When the burial took place) he took a vow to the effect that by the time the robe was exhumed he would be reincarnated as the abbot of the monastery, and also that he would undertake to renovate the shrine and the building.

A bhikkhu quoted the following stanza composed by Dhyana Master Wo Lun :

Wo Lun has ways and means
To insulate the mind from all thoughts.
When circumstances do not react on the mind
The Bodhi tree will grow steadily.

Hearing this, the Patriarch said, "This stanza indicates that the composer of it has not yet fully realised the Essence of Mind. To put its teaching into practice (would gain no liberation), but bind oneself more tightly." Thereupon, he showed the Bhikkhu the following stanza of his own :

Hui Neng has no ways and means
To insulate the mind from all thoughts.
Circumstances often react on my mind,
And I wonder how can the Bodhi tree grow ?

Note.—In the last line the Patriarch challenged the statement that "the Bodhi tree will grow," as Bodhi neither increases nor decreases.

CHAPTER VIII

*THE SUDDEN SCHOOL AND THE GRADUAL SCHOOL**

WHILE the Patriarch was living in Pao Lin Monastery, the Grand Master Shen Hsiu was preaching in Yü Chüan Monastery of Ching Nan. At that time the two Schools, that of Hui Neng of the South and Shen Hsiu of the North, flourished side by side. As the two Schools were distinguished from each other by the names "Sudden" (the South) and "Gradual" (the North), the question which sect they should follow baffled certain Buddhist scholars (of that time).

(Seeing this), the Patriarch addressed the assembly as follows :

"So far as the Dharma is concerned, there can be only one School. (If a distinction exists) it exists in the fact that the founder of one school is a northern man, while the other is a southerner. While there is only one Dharma, some disciples realise it more quickly than others. The reason why the names 'Sudden' and 'Gradual' are given is that some disciples are superior to others in mental disposi-

* Note by Mr. Dwight Goddard.

When Hui Neng was at the Patriarch's monastery at Huang Mei, the Master (or Dean as we should call him) was Shen Hsiu, a notably learned monk of the Dhyana School. After Hui Neng left Huang Mei he lived in retirement for a number of years, but in disappointment at not receiving the appointment of Sixth Patriarch, returned to his home in the North and founded his own School which later, under Imperial patronage, came into great prominence. After the death of Shen Hsiu the School steadily lost prestige, and later dropped out of importance. But the different principles of the two schools, "Sudden Enlightenment" of the Sixth Patriarch's Sudden School, and "Gradual Attainment" of Shen Hsiu's Northern School, have continued to divide Buddhism and do so today. The principle in dispute is whether enlightenment comes as a gradual attainment, through study of the scriptures and the practice of dhyana or, as the Japanese say, it comes in some sudden and convincing "satori." It is not a question of quickness or slowness in arriving at it ; "gradual attainment" may arrive sooner than "sudden enlightenment." It is the question whether enlightenment comes as the culmination of a gradual process of mental growth, or whether it is a 'sudden turning at the seat of consciousness' from an habitual reliance on the thinking faculty (a looking outward) to a new use of a higher intuitive faculty (a looking inward).

tions. So far as the Dharma is concerned, the distinction of 'Sudden' and 'Gradual' does not exist."

(In spite of what the Patriarch had said,) the followers of Shen Hsiu used to criticise the Patriarch. They discredited him by saying that as he was illiterate he could not distinguish himself in any respect.

Shen Hsiu himself, on the other hand, admitted that he was inferior to the Patriarch, that the Patriarch attained wisdom without the aid of a teacher, and that he understood thoroughly the teaching of the Mahayana School. "Moreover," he added, "my teacher, the Fifth Patriarch, would not have transmitted to him the robe and the bowl without good cause. I regret that, owing to the patronage of the state, which I by no means deserve, I am unable to travel far to receive instructions from him personally. (But) you men should go to Ts'ao Ch'i to consult him,"

One day he said to his disciple, Chi Ch'êng, "You are intelligent and bright. On my behalf, you may go to Ts'ao Ch'i to attend the lectures there. Try your best to remember what you learn, so that upon your return you may repeat it to me."

Acting on his teacher's instruction, Chi Ch'êng went to Ts'ao Ch'i. Without telling whence he came he joined the crowd there to call on the Patriarch.

"Some one has hidden himself here to plagiarize my lecture," said the Patriarch to the assembly. Thereupon, Chi Ch'êng came out, made obeisance, and told the Patriarch what his mission was.

"You come from Yü Ch'üan Monastery, do you?" asked the Patriarch. "You must be a spy."

"No, I am not," replied Chi Ch'êng.

"Why not?" asked the Patriarch.

"If I had not told you," said Chi Ch'êng, "I would be a spy. Since I have told you all about it, I am not."

"How does your teacher instruct his disciples?" asked the Patriarch.

"He tells us to meditate on purity, to keep up the sitting

position all the time and not to lie down," replied Chi Ch'êng.

"To meditate on purity," said the Patriarch, "is an infirmity and not Dhyana. To restrict oneself to the sitting position all the time is unprofitable. Listen to my stanza :

"A living man sits and does not lie down (all the time),
While a dead man lies down and does not sit.
On this physical body of ours
Why should we impose the task of sitting ?"

Making obeisance a second time, Chi Ch'êng remarked, "Though I have studied Buddhism for nine years under the Grand Master Shen Hsiu, my mind has not yet been awakened for enlightenment. But as soon as you speak to me my mind is enlightened. As the question of incessant re-births is a momentous one, please take pity on me and give me further instruction."

"I understand," said the Patriarch, "that your teacher gives his disciples instructions on Sila (disciplinary rules), Dhyana (meditation), and Prajna (Wisdom). Please tell me how he defines these terms."

"According to his teaching," replied Chi Ch'êng "to refrain from all evil actions is Sila, to practise whatever is good is Prajna, and to purify one's own mind is Dhyana. This is the way he teaches us. May I know your system? "

"If I tell you," said the Patriarch, "that I have a system of Law to transmit to others, I am cheating you. What I do to my disciples is to liberate them from their own bondage with such devices as the case may need. To use a name which is nothing but a makeshift, this (state of liberation) may be called Samadhi. The way your master teaches Sila, Dhyana, and Prajna is wonderful ; but my exposition is different."

"How can it be different, Sir," asked Chi Ch'êng, "when there is only one form of Sila, Dhyana and Prajna ?"

"The teaching of your master," replied the Patriarch,

"is for the guidance of the followers of the Mahayana School, while mine is for those of the Supreme School. The fact that some realise the Dharma more quickly and deeply than others accounts for the difference in the interpretation. You may listen, and see if my instruction is the same as his. In expounding the Law, I do not deviate from the authority of the Essence of Mind (*i.e.*, I speak what I realise intuitively). To speak otherwise would indicate that the speaker's Essence of Mind is under obscuration and that he can touch the phenomenal side of the Law only. The true teaching of Sila, Dhyana, and Prajna should be based on the principle that the function of all things derives from the Essence of Mind. Listen to my stanza :

"To free the mind from all impurity is the Sila of the Essence of Mind.
To free the mind from all disturbance is the Dhyana of the Essence of Mind.
That which neither increases nor decreases is the Diamond (used as a symbol for the Essence of Mind) ;
'Coming' and 'going' are different phases of Samadhi."

Having heard this, Chi Ch'êng apologised (for having asked a foolish question) and thanked the Patriarch for his instruction.
He then submitted the following stanza :

The 'self' is nothing but a phantasm created by the union of five skandhas,
And a phantasm can have nothing to do with absolute reality.
To hold that there is Tathata (Suchness) for us to aim at or to return to
Is another example of 'Impure Dharma.'*

Approving what he said in his stanza, the Patriarch said to him again, "The teaching of your master on Sila, Dhyana, and Prajna applies to wise men of the inferior type, while

* For Pure Law is above concept and speech.

mine to those of the superior type. He who realises the Essence of Mind may dispense with such doctrines as Bodhi, Nirvana, and 'Knowledge of Emancipation.' Only those who do not possess a single system of Law can formulate all systems of Law, and only those who can understand the meaning (of this paradox) may use such terms. It makes no difference to those who have realised the Essence of Mind whether they formulate all systems of Law or dispense with all of them. They are at liberty to 'come' or to 'go' (*i.e.*, they may remain in or leave this world at their own free will). They are free from obstacles or impediments. They take appropriate actions as circumstances require. They give suitable answers according to the temperament of the enquirer. They see that all Nirmanakayas are one with the Essence of Mind. They attain liberation, psychic powers and Samadhi, which enable them to perform the arduous task of universal salvation, as easily as if they were only playing. Such are the men who have realised the Essence of Mind !"

"By what principle are we guided in dispensing with all systems of Law ?" was Chi Ch'êng's next question.

"When our Essence of Mind is free from impurity, infatuations and disturbances," replied the Patriarch, "when we introspect our mind from moment to moment with Prajna, and when we do not cling to things and phenomenal objects we are free and liberated. Why should we formulate any system of Law when our goal can be reached no matter whether we turn to the right or to the left ? Since it is with our own efforts that we realise the Essence of Mind, and since the realisation and the practice of the Law are both done instantaneously, and not gradually or stage by stage, the formulation of any system of Law is unnecessary. As all Dharmas are intrinsically Nirvanic, how can there be gradation in them ?"

Chi Ch'êng made obeisance and volunteered to be an attendant of the Patriarch. In that capacity, he served both day and night.

Bhikkhu Chih Ch'ê, whose secular name was Chang Hsing-Ch'ang, was a native of Kiangsi. As a young man, he was fond of chivalric exploits.

Since the two Dhyana Schools, Hui Neng of the South and Shen Hsiu of the North, flourished side by side, a strong sectarian feeling ran high on the part of the disciples, in spite of the tolerant spirit shown by the two masters. As they called their own teacher, Shen Hsiu, the Sixth Patriarch on no better authority than their own, the followers of the Northern School were jealous of the rightful owner of that title whose claim, supported by the inherited robe, was too well known to be ignored. (So in order to get rid of the rival teacher) they sent Chang Hsing-Ch'ang (who was then a layman) to murder the Patriarch.

With his psychic power of mind-reading the Patriarch was able to know of the plot beforehand. (Making ready for the coming of the murderer), he put ten taels by the side of his own seat. Chang duly arrived, and one evening entered the Patriarch's room to carry out the murder. With outstretched neck the Patriarch waited for the fatal blow. Thrice did Chang cut, (but) not a single wound was thereby inflicted ! The Patriarch then addressed him as follows :

> "A straight sword is not crooked,
> While a crooked one is not straight.
> I owe you money only ;
> But life I do not owe."

The surprise was too great for Chang ; he fell into a swoon and did not revive for a considerable time. Remorseful and penitent, he asked for mercy and volunteered to join the Order at once. Handing him the money, the Patriarch said, "You had better not remain here, lest my followers should do you harm. Come to see me in disguise some other time, and I will take good care of you."

As directed, Chang ran away the same night. Subsequently, he joined the Order and, when fully ordained, proved himself to be a very diligent monk.

One day, recollecting what the Patriarch had said, he took the long journey to see him and to tender him homage. "Why do you come so late?" asked the Patriarch. "I have been thinking of you all the time."

"Since that day you so graciously pardoned my crime," said Chang, "I have become a bhikkhu and have studied Buddhism diligently. Yet I find it difficult to requite you adequately unless I can show my gratitude by spreading the Law for the deliverance of sentient beings. In studying the Maha Parinirvana Sutra, which I read very often, I cannot understand the meaning of 'eternal' and 'not eternal.' Will you, Sir, kindly give me a short explanation."

"What is not eternal is the Buddha-nature," replied the Patriarch, "and what is eternal is the discriminating mind together with all meritorious and demeritorious Dharmas."

"Your explanation, Sir, contradicts the Sutra," said Chang.

"I dare not, since I inherit the 'Heart-Seal' of Lord Buddha," replied the Patriarch.

"According to the Sutra," said Chang, "the Buddha-nature is eternal, while all meritorious and demeritorious Dharmas, including the Bodhi-citta (the Wisdom-heart) are not eternal. As you hold otherwise, is this not a contradiction? Your explanation has now intensified my doubts and perplexities."

"On one occasion," replied the Patriarch, "I had Bhik-khuni Wu Ching-Ts'ang recite to me the whole book of the Maha Parinirvana Sutra, so that I could explain it to her. Every word and every meaning I explained on that occasion agreed with the text. As to the explanation I give you now, it likewise differs not from the text."

"As my capacity for understanding is a poor one," observed Chang, "will you kindly explain to me more fully and more clearly."

"Don't you understand?" said the Patriarch. "If

Buddha-nature is eternal, it would be of no use to talk about meritorious and demeritorious Dharmas ; and until the end of a kalpa no one would arouse the Bodhi-citta. Therefore, when I say 'not-eternal' it is exactly what Lord Buddha meant for 'eternal.' Again, if all Dharmas are not eternal, then every thing or object would have a nature of its own (*i.e.*, positive essence) to suffer death and birth. In that case, it would mean that the Essence of Mind which is truly eternal does not pervade everywhere. Therefore when I say 'eternal' it is exactly what Lord Buddha meant by 'not-eternal.'

"Because ordinary men and heretics believe in 'heretical eternalism' (*i.e.*, they believe in the eternity of soul and of the world), and because sravakas (aspirants to arhatship) mistake the eternity of Nirvana as something not eternal, eight upside-down notions arise.* In order to refute these one-sided views, Lord Buddha preached in the Maha Parinirvana Sutra the 'Ultimate Doctrine' of Buddhist teaching, *i.e.*, true eternity, true happiness, true self, and true purity.

"In following slavishly the wording of the Sutra, you have ignored the spirit of the text. In assuming that what perishes is non-eternal and that what is fixed and immutable is eternal, you have misinterpreted Lord Buddha's dying instruction (contained in the Maha Parinirvana Sutra) which is perfect, profound, and complete. You may read the Sutra a thousand times but you will get no benefit out of it."

All of a sudden Chang awoke to full enlightenment, and submitted the following stanza to the Patriarch :

In order to refute the bigoted belief of 'Non-eternity'
Lord Buddha preached the 'Eternal Nature.'

---

* Ordinary men and heretics mistake the non-eternity, non-happiness, non-egoism, and non-purity of mundane existence for eternity, happiness, egoism, and purity ; while Sravakas mistake the Eternity, Happiness, Egoism and Purity of Nirvana for Non-eternity, Non-happiness, Non-egoism and Non-purity.

He who does not know that such preaching is only a skilful
    device
May be likened to the child who picks up pebbles and calls
    them gems.
Without effort on my part
The Buddha-nature manifests itself.
This is due neither to the instruction of my teacher
Nor to any attainment of my own.

"You have now thoroughly realised (the Essence of
Mind)," commended the Patriarch, "and hereafter you
should name yourself Chih Ch'ê (to realise thoroughly)."
Chih Ch'ê thanked the Patriarch, made obeisance, and
departed.

Note.—The Buddha's object is to get rid of bigoted belief in any form.
He would preach 'Non-eternity' to believers of Eternalism ; and preach
'neither Eternity nor Non-eternity' to those who believe in both.

A thirteen year old boy named Shen Hui, who was born
of a Kao family of Hsiang Yang, came from Yu Chuan
Monastery to tender homage to the Patriarch.

"My learned friend," said the Patriarch, "it must be hard
for you to undertake such a long journey.   But can you tell
me what is the 'fundamental principle' ?   If you can, you
know the owner (*i.e.*, the Essence of Mind).   Try to say
something, please."

"Non-attachment is the fundamental principle,* and to

* Manjusri asked Vimalakirti, "What is the source of our body ?"
"Craving and desire," answered Vimalakirti.
"What is the source of craving and desire ?"
"Delusion and particularization."
"What is the source of delusion and particularization ?"
"Topsy-turvy views."
"What is the source of topsy-turvy views ?"
"Non-attachment."
"What is the source of non-attachment ?"
"Non-attachment has no source, Manjusri.   With non-attachment as
basis, all Dharmas are established."

                                         Vimalakirti Nirdesa Sutra.

Commentary on the above by Dharma Master Seng Shao :
"If we take the 'action of the mind' as the source, then 'phenomena' would
exist.   But the 'Ultimate of the Norm' or the 'Primordial Action' has no

91

know the owner is to realise (the Essence of Mind)," replied Shen Hui.

"This novice is fit for nothing but to talk loosely," reproved the Patriarch.

Thereupon Shen Hui asked the Patriarch, "In your meditation, Sir, do you see (your Essence of Mind) or not ?"

Striking him three blows with his staff, the Patriarch asked him whether he felt pain or not. "Painful and not painful," replied Shen Hui. "I see and I see not," retorted the Patriarch.

"How is it that you see and see not ?" asked Shen Hui.

"What I see is my own faults," replied the Patriarch. "What I do not see is the good, the evil, the merit and the demerit of others. That is why I see and I see not. Now

---

source. If we take 'non-Dharma' as the source, then 'inexistence' would be the cause of 'inexistence.' But as 'inexistence' needs not another 'inexistence' to be its cause, it would also be sourceless."

Further, he said : "From Non-attachment topsy-turvy views arise. From topsy-turvy views, particularization arises. From particularization, craving and desire arise. From craving and desire, our physical body exists. The existence of our physical body will be ensued by good and evil elements from which all Dharmas arise. Thenceforth, things become so multifarious that neither speech nor enumeration can exhaust them."

According to Dharma Master Seng Shao, the primordial mind-impulse or the fundamental non-enlightenment is the source of Non-attachment. In the "Transmission of the Lamp," National Teacher Ch'ing Liang, in reply to the question put to him by the Crown Prince on the essential teaching of the mind, said, "The source of the ultimate teaching is the Transcendental Mind and the source of the Transcendental Mind is Non-attachment. The inherent quality of Non-attachment is omniscience and freedom from obscuration."

The quotation, "One should use one's mind in such a way that it will be free from any attachment," from the Diamond Sutra expresses the same idea.

In his book, *An Explicit Treatise on Dhyana Teaching*, Dhyana Master Ho Tsê said, "After the Parinirvana of the Exalted One, the twenty eight Patriarchs of India all transmitted the 'Mind of Non-attachment' to their successors. What is referred to as 'Non-attachment' is the real state of all things (*i.e.*, things as they really are, things stripped of their draperies and trappings). In such a state, truth and falsehood merge into one. Call it 'unity,' it is of many kinds. Call it 'duplicity,' it is non-dualistic."

From the above, it will be seen that this sentence, "Non-attachment is the fundamental principle," is the keynote of the Dhyana teaching.

DIH PING TSZE.

tell me what you mean by 'painful and not painful.' If you feel no pain, you would be as a piece of wood or stone. On the other hand, should you feel pain, and anger or hatred is thereby aroused, you would be in the same position as an ordinary man.

"The 'seeing' and 'not-seeing' you referred to are a pair of opposites ; while 'painful' and 'not painful' belong to conditioned Dharma which becomes and ceases. Without having realised your own Essence of Mind, you dare to hoodwink others."

Shen Hui apologised, made obeisance, and thanked the Patriarch for his instruction.

Addressing him again the Patriarch said, "If you are under delusion and cannot realise your Essence of Mind, you should seek the advice of a pious and learned friend. When your mind is enlightened, you will know the Essence of Mind, and then you may tread the Path the right way. Now you are under delusion, and do not know your Essence of Mind. Yet you dare to ask whether I know my Essence of Mind or not. If I do, I realise it myself, but the fact that I know it cannot help you from being under delusion. Similarly, if you know your Essence of Mind your knowing would be of no use to me. Instead of asking others, why not see it for yourself and know it for yourself ?"

Making obeisance more than a hundred times, Shen Hui gain expressed regret and asked the Patriarch to forgive him. (Henceforth) he worked diligently as the Patriarch's attendant.

Addressing the assembly one day, the Patriarch said, "I have an article which has no head, no name nor appellation, no front and no back. Do any of you know it ?"

Stepping out from the crowd, Shen Hui replied, "It is the source of all Buddhas, and the Buddha-nature of Shen Hui."

"I have told you already that it is without name and appellation, and yet you call it 'Source of Buddhas' and 'Buddha-nature,' " reproved the Patriarch. "Even if you confine yourself in a mat shed for further study, you will be a

Dhyana scholar of second hand knowledge only (*i.e.*, knowledge from books and verbal authority instead of Knowledge obtained intuitively).

After the death of the Patriarch, Shen Hui left for Loyang, where he spread widely the teaching of the Sudden School. The popular work entitled 'An Explicit Treatise on Dhyana Teaching' was written by him. He is generally known by the name Dhyana Master Ho Tse (the name of his monastery).

Seeing that many questions were put to him in bad faith by followers of various Schools, and that a great number of such questioners had gathered around him, the Patriarch addressed them out of compassion as follows :

"A treader of the Path should do away with all thoughts, good as well as evil ones. It is merely as an expedient that the Essence of Mind is so called ; it cannot really be named by any name. This 'non-dual nature' is called the 'true nature,' upon which all Dharma systems of teaching are based. One should realise the Essence of Mind as soon as one hears of it."

Upon hearing this, every one made obeisance and asked the Patriarch to allow them to be his disciples.

CHAPTER IX

ROYAL PATRONAGE

AN edict dated the 15th day of the 1st Moon of the 1st year of Shen Lung, issued by the Empress Dowager Tse T'ien and the Emperor Chung Tsung ran as follows :

"Since we invited Grand Masters Hui An and Shen Hsiu to stay in the palace to receive our offerings, we have studied the 'Buddha Vehicle' under them whenever we could find time after attending to our imperial duties. Out of sheer modesty, these two Masters recommended that we should seek the advice of Dhyana Master Hui Neng of the South, who had esoterically inherited the Dharma and the robe of the Fifth Patriarch as well as the 'Heart Seal' of Lord Buddha.

"We hereby send Hsüeh Chien as the courier of this Edict to invite His Holiness to come, and trust His Holiness will graciously favour us with an early visit to the capital."

On the ground of illness, the Patriarch sent a reply to decline the royal invitation and asked to be allowed to spend his remaining years 'in the forest.'

"Dhyana experts in the capital," said Hsüeh Chien (when interviewing the Patriarch), "unanimously advise people to meditate in the sitting position to attain Samadhi. They say that this is the only way to realise the Norm,* and that it is impossible for any one to obtain liberation without going through meditation exercises. May I know your way of teaching, Sir ?"

"The Norm is to be realised by the mind," replied the Patriarch, "and does not depend on the sitting position. The Diamond Sutra says that it is wrong for any one to assert that the Tathagata comes or goes, sits or reclines. Why ? Because the Tathagata's 'Dhyana of Purity' implies neither coming from anywhere nor going to anywhere, neither becoming nor causing to be. All Dharmas are calm and void, and such is the Tathagata's 'Seat of Purity.' Strictly speaking, there is even no such thing as 'attainment' ;

*Tao. Ed.

why then should we bother ourselves about the sitting position ?"

"Upon my return," said Hsüeh Chien, "Their Majesties will certainly ask me to make a report. Will you, Sir, kindly give me some essential hints on your teaching, so that I can make them known not only to Their Majesties, but also to all Buddhist scholars in the capital ? As the flame of one lamp may kindle hundreds or thousands of others, so the ignorant will be enlightened (by your teaching), and light will produce light without end."

"The Norm implies neither light nor darkness," replied the Patriarch. "Light and darkness signify the idea of alternation. (It is not correct to say) that light will produce light without end, because there is an end, since light and darkness are a pair of opposites. The Vimalakirti Nirdesa Sutra says, 'The Norm has no comparison, since it is not a relative term'. "

"Light signifies wisdom," argued Hsüeh Chien, "and darkness signifies klesa (defilement). If a treader of the Path does not break up klesa with the force of wisdom, how is he going to free himself from the 'wheel of birth and death,' which is beginningless ?"

"Klesa is Bodhi," rejoined the Patriarch. "The two are the same and not different. To break up klesa with wisdom is the teaching of the Sravaka (Arhat) School and the Pratyeka Buddha School, the followers of which are of the 'Goat Vehicle' and 'Deer Vehicle' standard respectively. To those of superior mental dispositions such teaching would be of no use at all."

"What then, is the teaching of the Mahayana School ?" asked Hsüeh Chien.

"From the point of view of ordinary men," replied the Patriarch, "enlightenment and ignorance are two separate things. Wise men who realise thoroughly the Essence of Mind know that they are of the same nature. This same nature or non-dual nature is what is called the 'real nature,' which neither decreases in the case of ordinary men and ignorant persons, nor increases in the case of the enlightened sage ; which is not disturbed in a state of annoyance, nor calm in a state of Samadhi. It is neither eternal nor non-eternal ; it neither goes nor comes ; it is not to be found in the exterior, nor in the interior, nor in the space between the two. It is above existence and non-existence ; its nature and its phenomena are always in a state of 'Thusness'; it is permanent and immutable. Such is the Norm."

Hsüeh Chien asked, "You say that it is above existence and non-existence. How then do you differentiate it from the teaching of the heretics who teach the same thing ?"

"In the teaching of the heretics," replied the Patriarch, " 'non-existence' means the end of 'existence,' while 'existence' is used in contrast with 'non-existence.' What they mean by 'non-existence' is not actually annihilation and what they call 'existence' does not really exist. What I mean by 'above existence and non-existence' is this; intrinsically it exists not, and at the present moment it will not be annihilated. Such is the difference between my teaching and that of the heretics.

"If you wish to know the essential points of my teaching, you should free yourself from all thoughts, good ones as well as bad ; then your mind will be in a state of purity, calm and serene all the time, and its usefulness as manifold as the grains of sand in the Ganges."

The preaching of the Patriarch suddenly awoke Hsüeh Chien to full enlightenment. He made obeisance and bid the Patriarch adieu. Upon his return to the palace, he reported what the Patriarch had said to Their Majesties.

In that same year, on the 3rd day of the 9th Moon, an edict was issued commending the Patriarch in the following terms :

"On the ground of old age and poor health, the Patriarch declined our invitation to come to the capital. Devoting his life to the practice of Buddhism for our benefit, he is indeed the 'field of merit' of the nation. Like Vimalakirti, who recuperated in Vaisali, he widely spreads the Mahayana teaching, transmits the doctrine of the Dhyana School, and expounds the system of 'Non-dual' Law.

"Through the medium of Hsüeh Chien, to whom the Patriarch has imparted the 'Buddha-knowledge,' we are fortunate enough to have a chance to understand for ourselves the teaching of the Supreme Vehicle. This must be due to our accumulated merits and our 'root of goodness' planted in past lives ; otherwise, we should not be the contemporaries of His Holiness.

"In appreciation of the graciousness of the Patriarch, we present to him herewith a Mo Na robe* and a crystal bowl. The Prefect of Shao Chou is hereby ordered to renovate his monastery and to convert his old residence into a temple which is to be named 'Kuo En' (State Munificence)."

* A valuable Buddhist robe made in Korea.

CHAPTER X

HIS FINAL INSTRUCTIONS

ONE day the Patriarch sent for his disciples, Fa Hai, Chih Ch'eng, Fa Ta, Shen Hui, Chih Ch'ang, Chih Tung, Chih Ch'e, Chih Tao, Fa Chen, Fa Ju etc., and addressed them as follows :

"You men are different from the common lot. After my entering into Nirvana, each of you will be the Dhyana Master of a certain district. I am, therefore, going to give you some hints on preaching, so that you may keep up the tradition of our School.

"First mention the three categories of Dharmas, and then the thirty six 'pairs of opposites' in the activities (of the Essence of Mind). Then teach how to avoid the two extremes of 'coming in' or 'going out.' In all preaching, stray not from the Essence of Mind. Whenever a man puts a question to you, answer him in antonyms, so that a 'pair of opposites' will be formed, such as 'coming' and 'going.' When the interdependence of the two is entirely done away with there would be, in the absolute sense, neither 'coming' nor 'going.'

"The three categories of Dharmas are :
Skandhas (aggregates),
Ayatanas (places of meeting),
Dhatus (factors of consciousness).
The five Skandhas are :
rupa (matter), vedana (sensation), samjna (perception), samskara (tendencies of mind), and vijnana (consciousness).
The twelve Ayatanas are :

Six Sense Objects (external).   Six Sense Organs (internal).

Object of sight		Organ of sight	
,,	,, hearing	,,	,, hearing
,,	,, smell	,,	,, smell
,,	,, taste	,,	,, taste
,,	,, touch	,,	,, touch
,,	,, thought	,,	,, thought

The eighteen Dhatus are :

The six sense objects, six sense organs, and six recipient vijnanas.

"Since the Essence of Mind is the embodiment of all Dharmas, it is called the Alaya (Repository) Consciousness. But as soon as the process of thinking or reasoning is started, the Essence of Mind is transmuted into (various) vijnanas. When the six recipient vijnanas come into being, they perceive the six sense objects through the six 'doors' (of sense). Thus, the functioning of the eighteen dhatus derive their impetus from the Essence of Mind. Whether they function with an evil tendency or a good one depends upon what mood—good or evil—the Essence of Mind is in. Evil functioning is that of a common man, while good functioning is that of a Buddha. It is because there are 'pairs of opposites' inherent in the Essence of Mind that the functioning of the eighteen dhatus derive their impetus.

"The thirty-six 'Pairs of opposites' are :

Five external inanimate ones : Heaven and earth, sun and moon, light and darkness, positive element and negative element, fire and water.

Twelve Dharmalaksana (phenomenal objects) : Speech and dharma, affirmation and negation, matter and non-matter, form and without form, taints (impurity) and absence of taint, matter and void, motion and quiescence, purity and impurity, ordinary people and sages, the Sangha and the laity, the aged and the young, the big and the small. Nineteen pairs denoting the functioning of the Essence of Mind : Long and short, good and evil, infatuated and enlightened, ignorant and wise, perturbed and calm, merciful and wicked, abstinent (Sila) and indulgent, straight and crooked, full and empty, steep and level, klesa and Bodhi, permanent and transient, compassionate and cruel, happy and angry, generous and mean, forward and backward, existent and non-existent, Dharmakaya and physical body, Sambhogakaya and Nirmanakaya.

"He who knows how to use these thirty-six pairs realises the all-pervading principle which goes through the teaching of all Sutras. Whether he is 'coming in' or 'going out,' he is able to avoid the two extremes.

"In the functioning of the Essence of Mind and in conversation with others, outwardly we should free ourselves from attachment to objects, and inwardly, we should free ourselves from attachment to the idea of the Void. To believe in the reality of objects or in Nihilism results in fallacious views or intensified ignorance respectively.

"A bigoted believer in Nihilism blasphemes against the Sutras on the ground that literature (*i.e.*, the Buddhist Scriptures) is unnecessary (for the study of Buddhism). If that were so, then neither would it be right for us to speak, since speech forms the substance of literature. He would also argue that in the direct method (literally, the straight Path) literature is discarded. But does he appreciate that the two words 'is discarded' are also literature ? Upon hearing others recite the Sutras such a man would criticise the speakers as 'addicted to scriptural authority.' It is bad enough for him to confine this mistaken notion to himself, but in addition, he blasphemes against the Buddhist scriptures. You men should know that it is a serious offence to speak ill of the Sutras, for the consequence is grave indeed!

"He who believes in the reality of outward objects tries to seek the form (from without) by practising a certain system of doctrine. He may furnish spacious lecture-halls for the discussion of Realism or Nihilism, but such a man will not for numerous kalpas realise the Essence of Mind.

"We should tread the Path according to the teaching of the Law, and not keep our mind in a state of indolence, thereby creating obstacles to its understanding. To preach or to hear the Law without practising it gives occasion for the arising of heretical views. Hence, we should tread the Path according to the teaching of the Law, and in the dissemination of the Dharma we should not be influenced by the concept of the reality of objects.

101

"If you understand what I say, and make use of it in preaching, in practice, and in your daily life, you will grasp the distinguishing feature of our School.

"Whenever a question is put to you, answer it in the negative, if it is an affirmative one ; and vice versa. If you are asked about an ordinary man, tell the enquirer something about a sage ; and vice versa. From the correlation or interdependence of the two opposites the doctrine of the 'Mean' may be grasped. If all other questions are answered in this manner, you will not be far away from the truth.

"Supposing some one asks you what is darkness, answer him thus : Light is the hetu (root condition) and darkness is the pratyaya (conditions which bring about any given phenomenon). When light disappears, darkness appears. The two are in contrast to each other. From the correlation or interdependence of the two the doctrine of the 'Mean' arises.

"In this way all other questions are to be answered. To ensure the perpetuation of the aim and object of our School in the transmission of the Dharma to your successors, this instruction should be handed down from one generation to another."

In the 7th Moon of the year of Jên Tzü, the 1st year of T'ai Chi or Yen Ho Era, the Patriarch sent some of his disciples to Hsin Chou to have a shrine (stupa) built within the Kuo En monastery, with instructions that the work should be completed as soon as possible. Next year, when summer was well-nigh spent, the stupa was duly completed.

On the 1st day of the 7th Moon, the Patriarch assembled his disciples and addressed them as follows :

"I am going to leave this world by the 8th Moon. Should you have any doubts (on the doctrine) please ask me in time, so that I can clear them up for you. You may find no one to teach you after my departure."

The sad news moved Fa Hai and other disciples to tears. Shen Hui, on the other hand, remained unperturbed. Commending him, the Patriarch said, "Young Master Shen Hui is the only one here who has attained that state of mind which sees no difference in good or evil, knows neither sorrow nor happiness, and is unmoved by praise or blame. After so many years' training in this mountain, what progress have you made ? What are you crying for now ? Are you worrying for me because I do not know whither I shall go ? But I do know ; otherwise I could not tell you beforehand what will happen. What makes you cry is that you don't know whither I am going. If you did, there would be no occasion for you to cry. In Suchness there is neither coming nor going, neither becoming nor cessation. Sit down, all of you, and let me read you a stanza on reality and illusion, and on motion and quietude. Read it, and your opinion will accord with mine. Practise it, and you will grasp the aim and object of our School."

The assembly made obeisance and asked the Patriarch to let them hear the stanza, which read as follows :

In all things there is nothing real,
And so we should free ourselves from the concept of the reality of objects.
He who believes in the reality of objects
Is bound by this very concept, which is entirely illusive.
He who realises the Essence of Mind within himself
Knows that the 'True Mind' is to be sought apart from phenomena.
If one's mind is bound by illusive phenomena
Where is Reality to be found, when all phenomena are unreal ?
Sentient beings are mobile ;
Inanimate objects are stationary.
He who trains himself by exercise to be motionless
(Gets no benefit) other than making himself as still as an inanimate object.
Should you find true Immobility
There is Immobility within activity.

Immobility (like that of inanimate objects) is immobility (and
   not Dhyana),
And in inanimate objects the seed of Buddhahood is not to
   be found.
He who is adept in the discrimination of various Dharmalaksana
Abides immovably in the 'First Principle' (Nirvana).
Thus are all things to be perceived,
And this is the functioning of Tathata (Suchness).
Treaders of the Path,
Exert yourself and take heed
That as followers of the Mahayana School
You do not embrace that sort of knowledge
Which binds you to the wheel of birth and death.
With those who are sympathetic
Let us have discussion on Buddhism.
As for those whose point of view differs from ours
Let us treat them politely and thus make them happy.
(But) disputes are alien to our School,
For they are incompatible with its doctrine.
To argue with others in disregard of this rule
Subjects one's Essence of Mind to the bitterness of mundane
   existence.

Having heard this stanza, the assembly made obeisance
in a body. In accordance with the wishes of the Patriarch,
they concentrated their minds to put the stanza into actual
practice, and refrained from religious controversy.

Seeing that the Patriarch would pass away in the near
future, the head Monk, Fa Hai, after prostrating himself
twice asked, "Sir, upon your entering into Nirvana, who
will be the inheritor of the robe of the Dharma ?"

"All my sermons," replied the Patriarch, "from the
time I preached in Ta Fan monastery, may be copied out
for circulation in a volume to be entitled 'Sutra Spoken on
the High Seat of the Treasure of the Law'. Take good care
of it and hand it down from one generation to another for
the salvation of all sentient beings. He who preaches in
accordance with its teachings preaches the Orthodox
Dharma.

"As to the transmission of the robe, this practice is to be

discontinued. Why? Because you all have implicit faith in my teaching, and being free from all doubts you are able to carry out the lofty object of our School. Furthermore, according to the implied meaning of the stanza by Bodhiharma, the first Patriarch, on the transmission of the Dharma, the robe need not be handed down. The stanza reads :

The object of my coming to this land (i.e., China)
Is to transmit the Dharma for the deliverance of those under delusion.
In five petals the flowers will be complete.
Thereafter, the fruit will come to bearing naturally.

The Patriarch added, "Learned Audience, purify your minds and listen to me. He who wishes to attain the All-knowing Knowledge of a Buddha should know the 'Samadhi of Specific Object' and the 'Samadhi of Specific Mode.' In all circumstances we should free ourselves from attachment to objects, and our attitude towards them should be neutral and indifferent. Let neither success nor failure, neither profit nor loss, worry us. Let us be calm and serene, modest and accommodating, simple and dispassionate. Such is the 'Samadhi of Specific Object.' On all occasions, whether we are standing, walking, sitting or reclining, let us be absolutely straightforward. Then, remaining in our sanctuary, and without the least movement, we shall virtually be in the Kingdom of Pure Land. Such is the 'Samadhi of Specific Mode.'

"He who is complete with these two forms of Samadhi may be likened to the ground with seeds sown therein. Covered up in the mud, the seeds receive nourishment therefrom and grow until the fruit comes into bearing.

"My preaching to you now may be likened to the seasonable rain which brings moisture to a vast area of land. The Buddha-nature within you may be likened to the seed which, being moistened by the rain, will grow rapidly. He who carries out my instructions will certainly attain Bodhi. He who follows my teaching will certainly attain the superb fruit (of Buddhahood). Listen to my stanza :

105

"Buddha-seeds latent in our mind
Will sprout upon the coming of the all-pervading rain.
The flower of the doctrine having been intuitively grasped,
One is bound to reap the fruit of Enlightenment."

Then he added, "The Dharma is non-dual and so is the mind. The Path is pure and above all forms. I warn you not to use those exercises for meditation on quietude or for keeping the mind a blank. The mind is by nature pure, so there is nothing for us to crave for or give up. Do your best, each of you, and go wherever circumstances lead."

Thereupon the disciples made obeisance and withdrew.

On the 8th day of the 7th Moon, the Patriarch gave a sudden order to his disciples to get ready a boat for Hsin Chou (his native place). In a body they entreated him earnestly and pitifully to stay.

"It is only natural that I should go," said the Patriarch, "for death is the inevitable outcome of birth, and even the various Buddhas who appear in this world have to go through an earthly death before entering Nirvana. There can be no exception for my physical body, which must be laid down somewhere."

"After your visit to Hsin Chou," entreated the assembly, "please return here sooner or later."

"Fallen leaves go back to where the root is, and when I first came I had no mouth," replied the Patriarch.*

Then they asked, "To whom, Sir, do you transmit the Womb of the Dharma Eye?"

"Men of principle will get it, and those who are mind-less will understand it."

They further asked, "Will any calamity befall you hereafter?"

"Five or six years after my death," replied the Patriarch, "a man will come to cut off my head. I have made the following prophecy of which please take note :

*Charles Luk suggests this means that the Essence of Mind is speechless ; in truth there is no Dharma that can be taught. Ed.

106

"To the top of the parent's head, offerings are made,
For the mouth must be fed.
When the calamity of 'Man' befalls,
Yang and Liu will be the officials."

He added, "Seventy years after my departure two Bodhisattvas from the East, one a layman and the other a monk, will preach contemporaneously, disseminate the Law widely, establish our School on a firm basis, renovate our monasteries and transmit the doctrine to numerous successors."

"Can you let us know for how many generations the Dharma has been transmitted, from the appearance of the earliest Buddha up to now ?" asked the disciples.

"The Buddhas who have appeared in this world are too many to be counted," replied the Patriarch.   "But let us start from the last seven Buddhas.   They are :

> BuddhaVipasyin
> Buddha Sikhin   of the last kalpa, the
> Buddha Visvabhu   Alamkarakalpa.

> Buddha Krakucchandha
> Buddha Kanakamuni   of the present kalpa,
> Buddha Kasyapa   the Bhadrakalpa.
> Buddha Sakyamuni

"From Buddha Sakyamuni, the Law was transmitted to the :

> 1st Patriarch Arya Mahakasyapa.
>   (It was then in turn transmitted to)
> 2nd Patriarch Arya Ananda
> 3rd   ,,   ,,   Sanakavasa
> 4th   ,,   ,,   Upagupta
> 5th   ,,   ,,   Dhritaka
> 6th   ,,   ,,   Michaka
> 7th   ,,   ,,   Vasumitra
> 8th   ,,   ,,   Buddhanandi
> 9th   ,,   ,,   Buddhamitra
> 10th   ,,   ,,   Parsva

11th Patriarch	Arya Punyayasas
12th ,,	Bodhisattva Asvaghosa
13th ,,	Arya Kapimala
14th ,,	Bodhisattva Nagarjuna
15th ,,	Kanadeva
16th ,,	Arya Rahulata
17th ,,	,, Sanghanandi
18th ,,	,, Gayasata
19th ,,	,, Kumarata
20th ,,	,, Jayata
21st ,,	,, Vasubandhu
22nd ,,	,, Manorhita
23rd ,,	,, Haklenayasas
24th ,,	,, Simha
25th ,,	,, Basiasita
26th ,,	,, Punyamitra
27th ,,	,, Prajnatara
28th ,,	Arya Bodhidharma (the 1st Patriarch in China)
29th ,,	Grand Master Hui K'u
30th ,,	,, ,, Seng Ts'an
31st ,,	,, ,, Tao Hsin
32nd ,,	,, ,, Hung Yen

And I am the 33rd Patriarch (the 6th Patriarch in China). Thus, the Dharma was handed down from one Patriarch to another. Hereafter, you men should in turn transmit it to posterity, from one generation to another, so that the tradition may be maintained.

On the 3rd day of the 8th Moon of the year of Kuei Chou, the 2nd Year of Hsien T'ien Era (A.D. 713), after taking food at the Kuo En Monastery, the Patriarch addressed his disciples as follows :

"Please sit down, for I am going to say good-bye."

Thereupon Fa Hai spoke to the Patriarch, "Sir, will you please leave to posterity definite instructions whereby people under delusion may realise the Buddha nature."

"It is not impossible," replied the Patriarch, "for these men to realise the Buddha-nature, provided they acquaint themselves with the nature of ordinary sentient beings. But to seek Buddhahood without such knowledge would be in vain even if one shall spend aeons of time in the search.

"Now, let me show you how to get acquainted with the nature of the sentient beings within your mind, and thereby realise the Buddha-nature latent in you. Knowing Buddha means nothing else than knowing sentient beings, for the latter ignore that they are potential Buddhas, whereas a Buddha sees no difference between himself and other beings. When sentient beings realise the Essence of Mind, they are Buddhas. If a Buddha is under delusion in his Essence of Mind, he is then an ordinary being. Purity in the Essence of Mind makes ordinary beings Buddhas. With impurity in the Essence of Mind even a Buddha is an ordinary being. When your mind is crooked or depraved, you are ordinary beings with Buddha-nature latent in you. On the other hand, when you direct your mind to purity and straightforwardness even for one moment, you are a Buddha.

"Within our mind there is a Buddha, and that Buddha within is the real Buddha. If Buddha is not to be sought within our mind, where shall we find the real Buddha ? Doubt not that Buddha is within your mind, apart from which nothing can exist. Since all things or phenomena are the production of our mind, the Sutra says, 'When mental activity begins, things come into being ; when mental activity ceases, they too cease to exist.' In parting from you, let me leave you a stanza entitled 'The Real Buddha of the Essence of Mind.' People of future generations who understand its meaning will realise the Essence of Mind and attain Buddhahood. It reads :

"The Essence of Mind or Tathata (Suchness) is the real Buddha,
While heretical views and the three poisonous elements are Mara.
Enlightened by Right Views, we call forth the Buddha within us.
When our nature is dominated by the three poisonous elements
We are said to be possessed by Mara ;

109

But when Right Views eliminate from our mind these poisonous
   elements
Mara will be transformed into a real Buddha.
The Dharmakaya, the Sambhogakaya and the Nirmanakaya—
These three Bodies emanate from one (the Essence of Mind).
He who is able to realise this fact intuitively
Has sown the seed, and will reap the fruit of Enlightenment.
It is from the Nirmanakaya that our Pure Nature emanates ;
Within the former the latter is to be found.
Guided by Pure Nature, the Nirmanakaya treads the Right
   Path,
And will some day attain to the Sambhogakaya, perfect and
   infinite.
'Pure Nature' is an outgrowth of our sensual instincts ;
By getting rid of sensuality, we attain the Pure Dharmakaya.
When our temperament is such that we are no longer the
   slaves of the five sense-objects,
And when we have realised the Essence of Mind even for one
   moment only, then Truth is known to us.
Should we be so fortunate as to be the followers of the Sudden
   School in this life,
In a sudden we shall see the Bhagavat of our Essence of Mind.
He who seeks the Buddha (from without) by practising certain
   doctrines
Knows not where the real Buddha is to be found.
He who is able to realise the Truth within his own mind
Has sown the seed of Buddhahood.
He who has not realised the Essence of Mind and seeks the
   Buddha from without
Is a fool motivated by wrong desires.
I have hereby left to posterity the teaching of the Sudden
   School
For the salvation of all sentient beings who care to practise it.
Hear me, ye future disciples !
Your time will have been badly wasted if you neglect to put
   this teaching into practice."

Having recited the stanza, he added, "Take good care of
yourselves. After my passing away, do not follow the
worldly tradition, and cry or lament. Neither should
messages of condolence be accepted, nor mourning be worn.

These things are contrary to the Orthodox Teaching, and he who does them is not my disciple. What you should do is to know your own mind and realise your own Buddha-nature, which neither rests nor moves, neither becomes nor ceases to be, neither comes nor goes, neither affirms nor denies, neither stays nor departs. Lest your mind should be under delusion and thus fail to catch my meaning, I repeat this to you to enable you to realise your Essence of Mind. After my death, if you carry out my instructions and practise them accordingly, my being away from you will make no difference. On the other hand, if you go against my teaching, no benefit would be obtained, even if I continued to stay here."

Then he uttered another stanza :

Imperturbable and serene the ideal man practises no virtue.
Self-possessed and dispassionate, he commits no sin.
Calm and silent, he gives up seeing and hearing.
Even and upright his mind abides nowhere.

Having uttered the stanza, he sat reverently until the third watch of the night. Then he said abruptly to his disciples, "I am going now," and in a sudden passed away. A peculiar fragrance pervaded his room, and a lunar rainbow appeared which seemed to join up earth and sky. The trees in the wood turned white, and birds and beasts cried mournfully.

In the 11th Moon of that year the question of the Patriarch's resting place gave rise to a dispute among the government officials of Kuang Chow, Shao Chou and Hsin Chou, each party being anxious to have the remains of the Patriarch removed to its own district. The Patriarch's disciples, together with other monks and laymen, took part in the controversy. Being unable to come to any settlement among themselves, they burnt incense and prayed to the Patriarch to indicate by the direction of the drift of the smoke the place which he himself would choose. As the smoke turned directly to Ts'ao Ch'i, the shrine (in which the body

111

was kept) together with the inherited robe and bowl was accordingly taken back there on the 13th day of the 11th Moon.

Next year, on the 25th day of the 7th Moon, the body was taken out of the shrine, and Fang Pien, a disciple of the Patriarch, plastered it with incense-clay. Recollecting the Patriarch's prediction that some one would take away his head, the disciples, as a matter of precaution, strengthened his neck by wrapping it with iron sheets and lacquered cloth before the body was placed into the stupa. Suddenly, a flash of white light rushed out from the stupa, went straight towards the sky, and did not disperse until three days after. The incident was duly reported to the Throne by the officials of Shao Chou District. By imperial order, tablets were erected to record the life of the Patriarch.

The Patriarch inherited the robe when he was 24, had his hair shaved (i.e., was ordained) at 39, and died at the age of 76. For thirty-seven years he preached for the benefit of all sentient beings. Forty-three of his disciples inherited the Dharma, and by his express consent became his successors, while those who attained enlightenment and thereby got out of the rut of the ordinary man were too numerous to be counted.

The robe transmitted by Bodhidharma as the insignia of Patriarchship, the Mo Na robe and the crystal bowl presented by Emperor Chung Tsung, the Patriarch's statue made by Fang Pien, and other sacred articles, were put in charge of the keeper of the stupa. They were to be kept permanently in Pao Lin Monastery to guard the welfare of the temple. The Sutra spoken by the Patriarch was published and circulated to make known the principles and objects of the Dharma School. All these steps were taken for the prosperity of the Three Gems (i.e., Buddha, Law, and Order) as well as for the general welfare of all sentient beings.

END OF THE SUTRA

APPENDIX BY LING T'AO, THE STUPA KEEPER

At midnight of the 3rd day of the 8th Moon of the Year of Jen Hsü, in the 10th year of the K'ai Yüan Era (A.D. 722), noises similar to those made by the dragging of an iron chain were heard within the stupa in which the Patriarch's remains were enshrined. Awakened by the alarm, the monks saw a man in mourning run out from the pagoda. Subsequently, they found that injuries had been inflicted on the Patriarch's neck. Reports were duly made to Prefect Liu Wu-T'ien and Magistrate Yang K'an. Upon receiving the complaint they made a vigilant search for the culprit, who five days after was arrested in Shih Chüeh Village and sent to Shao Chou for trial.

He stated that his name was Chang Chin-Man, a native of Liang Hsien of Ju Chou, and that in K'ai Yüan Monastery of Hung Chou he had received two thousand cash from a Hsin Lo (a state in Korea) monk named Chin Ta-Pei, who ordered him to steal the Patriarch's head to be sent back to Korea for veneration.

Having taken this statement Prefect Liu reserved judgment, and went personally to Ts'ao Ch'i to consult the Patriarch's senior disciple, Ling T'ao, as to the sentence to be passed. Ling T'ao said, "According to the law of the state, the death sentence should be passed. But as mercy is the keynote of Buddhism, which teaches that kindred and enemies should be treated alike, coupled with the fact that religious veneration is the motive for the crime, the offender may be pardoned." Much impressed, Prefect Liu exclaimed, "Now I begin to realise how liberal and broad-minded the Buddhists are !" The prisoner was accordingly set free.

Emperor Su Tsung, who wished to do veneration to the Patriarch's robe and bowl, sent an ambassador to Ts'ao Ch'i to escort them with due respect to the royal palace. They were kept there until the 1st Year of Yung T'ai (A.D. 765), when Emperor Tai Tsung had a dream in the night of the 5th day of the 5th Moon that the Patriarch asked him to return the relics. On the 7th day of the same moon, the following edict addressed to Yang Chien was issued :

"Whereas His Majesty dreamt that Dhyana Master Hui Neng asked for the restitution of the inherited robe and bowl, Marshal Chen Kuo ('Pillar of State,' a title of honour) Liu Ch'ung-Ching is hereby detailed to convey them with due reverence to Ts'ao Ch'i. These relics are regarded by His Majesty as state valuables, and you are directed to store them properly in Pao Lin Monastery and give express orders to the monks, who had received personal instructions from the Patriarch, to exercise special care for their protection, so that no loss or damage may be suffered."

Thereafter, the relics were stolen several times, but on each occasion they were recovered before the thief could run far away.

Emperor Hsien Tsung conferred on the Patriarch the Posthumous title 'Ta Chien' (the Great Mirror), and wrote the epigraph 'Yüan Ho Ling Chao' (Harmonious Spirit shines forth divinely) for the stupa.

Other biographical materials are to be found in the tablets recording the life of the Patriarch written by Chancellor Wang Wei, Prefect Liu Tzung-Yüan, Prefect Liu Yü-Hai and others, all of the Tang Dynasty.
